Elham V Way

Sentier de la Vallée d'Elham

C000282319

Acknowledgements

We are grateful to the following bodies and individuals for their assistance in route development and in the preparation of this guidebook:

   Canterbury City Council

   Parish Councils

   Kent County Council Highways and Transportation Department

   Forest Enterprise

   Kent Wildlife Trust

   Many local landowners and farmers

   Millgate Publishing

   Ministry of Defence - Defence Estate Organisation (Lands)

   Savills

   Shepway Footpath Preservation Society

   Canterbury Conservation Volunteers

   Kentish Stour Conservation Volunteers

   White Cliffs Countryside Volunteers

   Dr E P Allison (Canterbury Archaeological Trust)

   Tim Tatton-Brown

We give our special thanks to John Criddle who did a considerable amount of voluntary work towards the development of the Elham Valley Way. He leads a guided walk along the Way each year.

The development and promotion of the Elham Valley Way has been achieved with financial assistance from the Countryside Commission and Shepway District Council.

COUNTRYSIDE COMMISSION   **SHEPWAY DISTRICT COUNCIL**

Guidebooks in this series, also available:

   Darent Valley Path
   Eden Valley Walk
   Greensand Way
   High Weald Walk
   Medway Valley Walk
   Stour Valley Walk

Other route guidebooks are planned and in preparation.

Copies of these guidebooks can be obtained from bookshops, tourist information centres, libraries and post free from the Access and Recreation Officer, Kent County Council, Planning Department, Springfield, Maidstone, Kent ME14 2LX.

Along and Around the
Elham Valley
Way
Hythe - Canterbury

Sentier de la Vallée d'Elham
avec résumés en français

Produced and designed by the Countryside Group
and The Design Studio, Kent County Council

Authors - Brian Hart and Eila Lawton

Illustrators - John Cann and Philip Rutt

Photographer - Tim Fagan (except where indicated)

Maps produced by The Design Studio.
Reproduced from the Ordnance Survey mapping with
the permission of the Controller of Her Majesty's Stationery
Office © Crown copyright. Unauthorised reproduction
infringes Crown copyright and may lead to prosecution
or civil prodeedings.
Kent County Council LA 076708/97/03

Printed in Great Britain by County Print.

Published by Kent Environment & Planning Agency, Kent
County Council, Springfield, Maidstone, Kent ME14 2LX.

First edition May 1994
Second edition (updated and expanded), September 1997

Copyright © Kent Environment & Planning Agency

All rights reserved. No part of this publication
may be reproduced in any way without the written
permission of the publishers.

ISBN 1 873010 95 8

Contents
Sommaire

To the best of our knowledge the interpretive content and all other information is believed to be correct. We should be grateful if you would inform us of any changes, omissions or errors, so that modifications can be made in revisions of the book.

Elham Valley
Introduction

The Elham valley is the setting for the major part of this walk which will take you through some of the most enchanting countryside the garden county has to offer. From the seaside bustle of the south coast to the glories of the gracious city of Canterbury, the Elham Valley Way meanders through ancient woodlands, secret byways and charming, unspoilt villages. Much of the walk runs through the Kent Downs Area of Outstanding Natural Beauty and the Elham valley is acknowledged to be one of Kent's most precious natural assets.

Until the coming of the railway, the locality was reputedly known as the Nailbourne valley. The spring, which is the source of the Nailbourne, rises near Lyminge and flows northwards to eventually join the River Stour. Other tributaries emanating from the North Downs at Etchinghill run south to form the Seabrook Stream

which winds through an equally diverse landscape of softly undulating downs and deep valleys before it reaches the sea between Hythe and Sandgate. Whereas much of Britain's rural heritage has been swallowed up by modern development, the Elham valley has thankfully escaped such pressure and a sense of ordinary village life genuinely remains. This peaceful area of Kent contains something of interest for everyone. If you appreciate the

English landscape then you will never tire of many aspects along the way, be they the breath-taking panoramas around Folkestone and Hythe, or the wide variety of pastures, orchards, woods and parklands nearer Canterbury. If you are a naturalist then you will find plenty to detain you on the chalk downlands, whilst the ancient hedgerows and trees will fascinate you. Those of you who are curious about archaeology, ancient buildings,

View from Tolsford Hill

churches and all facets of architecture, will find the Elham valley rich with interest. Perhaps it goes without saying that should you be skilled in the art of painting and drawing, you will find more than enough to lure you to these parts again and again. If, however, you simply enjoy a thoroughly good walk then this appealing area can scarcely be bettered, no matter what season of the year you step out.

Only on foot may the Elham valley be fully appreciated providing many rewarding and memorable days out whether you complete the whole of the route or simply walk sections at a time. When you visit this beautiful corner of Kent and walk the Elham Valley Way, go at your own pace and savour its many sights, scents and sounds.

La vallée d'Elham sert de cadre à la majeure partie de cette randonnée qui vous emmènera à travers des paysages champêtres parmi les plus enchanteurs que puisse offrir le Jardin de l'Angleterre. Depuis le littoral sud et ses plages animées jusqu'aux splendeurs de l'élégante ville de Canterbury, l'Elham Valley Way serpente à travers des bois anciens, des chemins retirés et de charmants villages préservés. La majeure partie de la

Orchards in late summer

randonnée s'effectue dans le site naturel des Kent Downs, classé pour sa grande beauté. La vallée d'Elham est reconnue comme l'un des plus précieux atouts naturels du Kent.

Jusqu'à l'arrivée du chemin de fer, la région était connue sous le nom de vallée de Nailbourne. La rivière Nailbourne prend sa source près de Lyminge, coule vers le nord et rejoint la rivière Stour. D'autres cours d'eau émanant des North Downs à Etchinghill se jettent plus au sud dans la rivière Seabrook, qui serpente à travers un paysage tout aussi varié, composé de collines ondoyantes et de profondes vallées, avant d'atteindre la mer entre Hythe et Sandgate.

Contrairement à une grande partie du patrimoine rural de la Grande-Bretagne, envahi par les réalisations modernes, la vallée d'Elham a eu le bonheur d'échapper à ce sort; la simple vie de village y a conservé son charme. Cette paisible région du Kent a des attraits pour tous. Si

vous appéciez le paysage anglais, vous ne vous lasserez pas des nombreux points de vue qui s'offriront à vous en chemin, depuis les splendides panoramas de l'extrémité sud à la grande variété de prés, verges, bois et parcs plus près de Canterbury. Si vous êtes naturaliste dans l'âme, vous trouverez une quantité de raisons de vous attarder dans les collines crayeuses et serez fasciné par les haies et arbres anciens. Ceux d'entre vous qu'intéressent l'archéologie, les églises et édifices anciens et toutes les facettes de l'architecture seront amplement récompensés par la vallée d'Elham. Il va sans dire que si vous êtes doué pour la peinture ou le dessin, vous aurez là assez de sujets pour vous inciter à revenir. Si toutefois c'est le simple plaisir d'une randonnée qui vous attire,

il vous sera difficile de trouver mieux que cette région fascinante, et ce en toutes saisons.

La vallée d'Elham ne peut être pleinement appréciée qu'à pied. Elle vous offrira des journées mémorables que vous effectuiez la totalité de l'itinéraire ou en suiviez simplement certaines sections à la fois. Lorsque vous visiterez cette belle région du Kent au fil d'Elham Valley Way, marchez à votre rythme et savourez les nombreuses vue, senteurs et sonorités qui s'offrent à vous.

Kent Downs

Area of Outstanding Natural Beauty (AONB)

Areas of Outstanding Natural Beauty have been designated in the countryside since the 1949 National Parks and Access to the Countryside Act. The Kent Downs AONB was designated in 1968. Covering an area of 326 square miles (845 square kilometres), it is the fifth largest AONB in the country. Its wonderfully attractive mixture of open fields, sunken paths, colourful and diverse woodland, and chalk grassland rich in summer orchids and butterflies give it a unique quality. It faces some of the greatest pressures of all AONBs being in a relatively densely populated county, and because of its close proximity to the Continent there is pressure from developing transport networks.

North Elham

The eastern part of the Kent Downs is a remote, peaceful area of downland, which ends in the dramatic white cliffs of Dover. Above the southern scarp, the broad back of the chalk hills is furrowed by a series of long, narrow, parallel valleys, running north-east. In these dry valleys, the valley bottom streams (or winterbournes) are underground, only flowing at the surface occasionally, during very wet winters.

The western valley systems are more intricate. The steep, rounded slopes are crossed by thick shaws or overgrown hedges, often swathed in the white seed-heads of wild clematis. Large arable fields on the ridge-top plateaux are visually contained by long strips of deciduous, ancient woodland along the valley sides or ridge-top conifer forests, west of Elham. Towards the coast, however, the landscape becomes more exposed. There is less woodland and the strongly linear pattern of parallel ridges and valleys is more distinct.

In the Elham area the landscape changes between the remote, enclosed countryside east of the Stour valley and the exposed, severe ridges and valleys between

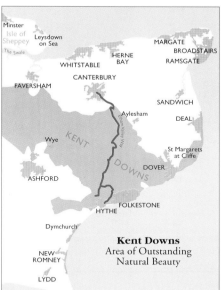

Kent Downs
Area of Outstanding
Natural Beauty

Folkestone and Dover. The Elham Valley carves its way through the centre of this area, in a wide attractive sweep, up to Barham and Patrixbourne. To the west lies a heavily wooded plateau, where expanses of conifer plantations are interspersed with remnants of deciduous ancient woodland, still concealing the ancient double banks, which once formed the boundary of Elham Park. This is one of the most densely wooded ridges of the AONB.

Folkestone lies at the most easterly end of the Greensand belt, on a narrow tongue of land contained by the downs in the north and the flat expanse

of Romney Marsh in the south. These physical constraints have resulted in a considerable amount of activity and development being confined within a small area on the very edge of the AONB.

The landscape here is dominated by major roads and the Channel Tunnel terminal, all of which are situated on the edge of the AONB between north Folkestone and the downs. Views from the scarp are of these developments and Folkestone has been severed from the AONB and its villages by the transport corridor. The scale of these developments, however, is matched by the dramatic landform of the steep, grassy scarp with its enclosed combes and prominent hills, which forms an impressive backdrop to the town and supports botanically-rich chalk grassland. The extraordinary conical shapes of the Sugarloaf Hill and Summerhouse Hill and the skyline earthworks of Castle Hill are key local landmarks.

A series of remote combes in the scarp towards Etchinghill overlook the now rare coppiced

Cottage, Patrixbourne

ash woodlands of Asholt Wood. Scrub extends up some of the lower slopes and thick hedges draws attention to the route of the Pilgrim's Way along the scarp-foot. Beyond this, the landscape is gently undulating, with large fields and substantial blocks of woodland.

Further south, around the outskirts of Hythe, this open, large-scale landscape gives way to a more intimate countryside of steep stream valleys, small woodlands and pasture.

Around Saltwood, the landscape takes on an enclosed character. There is a significant amount of deciduous woodland, especially along the valley sides, and the small pastures are surrounded by dense hedges and hedgerow trees. The towering gatehouse of Saltwood Castle, built in the ragstone from former quarries at Hythe, stands in a tiny area of ornamental parkland on the edge of a typical unspoilt valley. These little valleys bring valuable pockets of rural landscape up to the very edge of the town. The

high, open land above the Sene valley offers long views across the town and out to sea.

West of Tolsford Hill and Summerhouse Hill is a more open, intensively farmed agricultural landscape, which extends out of the AONB towards Ashford. Although the scarp is largely grassland, there are occasional blocks of deciduous woodland on the top, such as Brockman's Bushes on Tolsford Hill. These distinctive features draw the eye away from scarp-foot developments such as the motorways.

The most southerly part of the AONB extends from Hythe west to Aldington. The character area includes part of the Hythe escarpment, which

overlooks Romney Marsh. Until the early Middle Ages, this scarp formed the edge of a large, marshy lagoon. Gradually, however, the lagoon was reclaimed, through a combination of the natural accumulation of silt and shingle, the construction of sea defences and sustained drainage. The resulting land now forms one of the most fertile areas of Kent, with a particularly long growing season.

Most of the Hythe escarpment is the eroded face of the Greensand rocks and in particular of the calcareous Kentish ragstone. Over the centuries the surface has gradually slipped to form a steep, uneven slope, enclosing

the northern edge of the marsh. The vulnerability of the coast to attack has left a legacy of old military defences scattered across the area, from the tumbled walls of the Roman fort of Lemanis, to the 19th-century Royal Military Canal at the foot of the escarpment.

The scarp is highly visible from the flat marsh, forming a long hillside of rough grassland, dotted with scrub. Several large deciduous woodlands break up the sweep of the landform, being more characteristic in the west around Aldington. Between these woodlands, there are spectacular views across Romney Marsh and the English Channel.

The Hythe escarpment, unlike the chalk face of the downs, is furrowed throughout its length

Linseed

by small streams, which emerge from the sandstone, high up on the hillside and run down into the Royal Military Canal. To the east of the Port Lympne Wildlife Park, most of the scarp face is botanically rich rough grassland, with a considerable amount of scrub encroaching up the slopes. The sparse vegetation and the pitted, unstable soils produce a bleak, wild landscape, reflecting its exposed location.

Geology

The chalk outcrop of the Kent Downs forms part of the horseshoe of chalk which crosses south-east England.

Chalk is a relatively soft form of limestone laid down in a shallow sea 60-120 million years ago. The great uplift processes which produced the Alpine ranges of Europe 25 million years ago also created the geological dome of south-east England. Erosion by wind and water removed the central part of this dome, but because chalk is highly porous (it allows water to pass through it) it has remained to form upstanding hill ridges.

The downs are made up of a steep scarp slope, a plateau, and a gentle dip slope crossed by many dry valleys, rather like the branches of a tree. The dry valleys, of which the Elham valley is one (at least for most of the year), have been formed by stream erosion in wetter times.

The scarp slope runs in a north-westerly direction and is defined in this eastern section of the Kent Downs by Castle Hill, Sugarloaf Hill, Summerhouse Hill, and Tolsford Hill, all directly north of Folkestone and Hythe. The crest in this section reaches 185

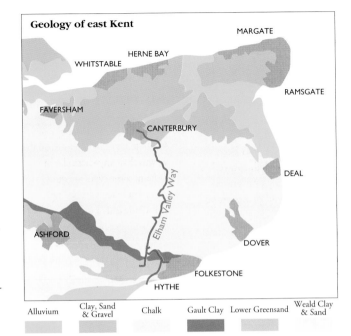

metres, providing some of the most impressive views in Kent.

The plateau areas are generally mantled with Plateau Drift or Clay-with-flints and these provide soils which make these chalk downs so different from those in Sussex, Hampshire, Wiltshire and Dorset where drift geology is largely absent. These soils are often very poor for agriculture and have therefore remained well-wooded.

The scarp slope of the downs is often shrouded in mist because of the sharp change in relief. It records some of the greatest rainfall in what is a particularly dry county.

This walk for the most part takes a route along the valley bottom of the Elham valley between Etchinghill and Canterbury. It also includes a section from the coast north across the belt of countryside between Hythe and Newington known as Holmesdale, then on to the base of the chalk escarpment of the North Downs at Coombe Farm and hence to Etchinghill at the top of the downland.

Outline geological section across the Downs and Weald

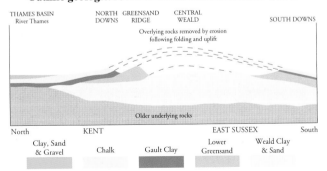

Elham valley

Chalk downland

Downland is chalk grassland, a pasture full of wildflowers. Along the Elham Valley Way you will discover, sometimes dramatic, sometimes gentle, chalk slopes where ancient downland has never been ploughed, seeded, sprayed or fertilised, only ever grazed, where the wild plants arrived naturally. In some cases the downland is many hundreds, perhaps even thousands of years old.

Thin soils over chalk, combined with the gentle influence of grazing, allow hundreds of wild flowers to grow while none gain dominance. Without grazing coarse grasses and scrub invade and overtop the delicate wildflowers; you can see where this is happening in many places along the way. Grazing is the traditional management of chalk downland.

Take a look in detail at the wonderful tapestry of ancient chalk grassland and you will find as many as 40 different species of wildflower or grass in a single square metre. This guidebook will highlight ancient chalk grassland along the route of the Elham Valley Way.

Plants which are still common on the downs include the cowslip in spring, along with milkwort, the scented wild thyme, marjoram and salad burnet, at Folkestone the summer ends with the gentle blues and mauves of hare bells, scabious and autumn gentian. Orchids are more plentiful on the downs than anywhere else in Britain, some types are quite common here; with spring comes the early purple orchid; early summer brings the fragrant, pyramidal and bee orchids.

The best known downland insects are the butterflies, some types such as the rare and dramatically beautiful Adonis blue live almost exclusively on downland. About half of the 60 or so species of butterfly found in the whole of Britain have been recorded on the Folkestone Downs.

The word downs is derived from the Celtic word dun which means a hill or fort. Paradoxically the downs are chalk hills.

Along the Elham Valley Way you will find references to early settlers on and around the downs. There are many tumuli (burial mounds) at Tolsford Hill and if you have a chance leave the path and follow the Downland Walk at Folkestone you can trace back history and enter the earthworks of a Norman castle along its original causeway.

Become a downland detective

As you walk along the Elham Valley Way, become a downland detective. By looking with care you can develop an eye for ancient downland. The first clue is often the land form, almost all of the ancient downland along the Way is found on land too steep to plough, look at the steep hills at Folkestone and along roads, ancient trackways or around old chalk quarries.

Not all grassland is all that green, well fertilised, sown grassland certainly is a bright, uniform green. Ancient downland will tend to be a more dull green in summer and a straw-like brownish green in winter.

Ant hills or other lumps and bumps in the grassland are a sure sign that the grassland has not been ploughed for many

Rape field, Etchinghill

years. Ant hills are built up over many decades, even centuries, and they die out if they become overshadowed by tall grasses or scrub.

Working landscape

All along the Elham Valley Way you can discover a working, evolving landscape. Passing from cattle and sheep grazing ancient downland, as they have for hundreds of years, you may then come across a newly coppiced woodland. Amongst the ancient landscape, there are many changes, old downland has been ploughed and now forms huge arable fields, old hedgerows are slowly declining from lack of management, old woods have been planted with pine and fir.

Part of this picture are the groups working to care for landscape, you can get involved and help farmers and the countryside projects manage special areas, contact any of the groups mentioned on the inside front cover with addresses on page 22.

Winterbournes

The Elham Valley Way follows a curious stream, the Nailbourne. The Nailbourne is a winterbourne, a seasonal chalk stream, its occasional flow has given rise to legends of woe and battles of good with evil.

Rain falling on the thin downland soils soon seeps underground through the porous chalk. Where the chalk meets underlying clay, springs develop. The stream may flow,

Folkestone Harbour

then disappear once more. The whole Nailbourne flows during wet winters, though some sections may be dry for years. Winterbournes are a typical feature of the chalk landscape and are important for wildlife. The fact they flow only occasionally makes them distinct and special.

Winterbournes are the home of animals and plants able to survive periods of drought and capable of colonising rapidly once water returns. See if you can find pond water-crowfoot

or fools water-cress at St Ethelburga's Well in Lyminge.

Ancient woodlands

Along the Elham Valley Way you pass through long-established villages, with medieval buildings. Also along the Way you pass through ancient woodlands, as individual and special as the villages, just like the villages, even the smallest wood will have its own name; you can find Ashley Wood and Thomas Acre Wood.

Woodland that can be traced back to the earliest accurate maps produced around 1600 is called ancient. Before this time woods were very rarely planted, the trees and shrubs arrived quite naturally, just as the wild

flowers in ancient chalk grassland. Very often ancient woodland is much older and may be a direct, though modified, descendent of the original wildwood that once covered most of Britain.

As a wildlife detective you will discover that such woodlands are carpeted with spring flowers. Bluebells, anemone, wild garlic, dogs mercury and woodland orchids are some of the plants that indicate to us that a woodland is ancient, these plants do not spread easily and are not found in great carpets in more modern plantations. Beware, sometimes an ancient site has been planted with trees that are not native to Britain, you may still find the remnants of the old wood under the dark canopy of pines and firs. Covert wood is part of a large site which has been replanted recently by the Forestry Commission.

Ancient woodland was a highly valued asset, providing building materials, charcoal, bark for tanning leather and fire wood, a sort of DIY centre and heating store. To protect the wood from grazing animals there was often a great wood bank dug in a sinuous line around the wood, like the special plants that will help us find ancient woods, a wood bank indicates that a woodland is old.

Most of the trees found in ancient woods will re-sprout if they are cut. This useful characteristic has been used over many centuries. Many stems grow from a cut stump, these can be used for poles, wattle in walls and sheep hurdles, fire wood and even pea sticks. Cutting tree stumps is called coppicing; many ancient woodlands are coppice woods.

Coppicing regularly in a wood keeps patches open allowing the sun in spring to bring on the wild flowers and woodland butterflies, a few years later the woodland becomes a thicket when it is perfect for nightingales to nest and dormice to scamper around. Coppice woods are cut on a

Chalk downland in spring, early purple orchids and cowslips

regular cycle of about 6-30 years depending what products are required. Much of the woodland wildlife relies on the ancient craft of the coppice woodsman.

Orchards

The deep rich brick earths and calcareous loams of north and east Kent, combined with a sunny climate, has enabled Kent to be the centre of British fruit production since the first orchard was planted in Teynham, near Faversham, in Henry VIII's time.

Orchards once covered much of the area around Canterbury, but most of the traditional orchards with their tall trees and wide crowns have now been grubbed and replaced with arable fields or dwarf rootstock fruit trees. These smaller trees crop heavily and are more easily picked, and are generally easier to manage. They still provide a spectacle of showy spring blossom even if they don't have the stature or elegance of the older trees.

Archaeology and history

The earliest foci of settlement occurred along the coastal plain and along Holmesdale, at Folkestone and Hythe. From these points there was easy access to the Continent. In the

Bronze Age, the Iron Age, and Roman and Viking periods, successive groups of invaders and raiders came and went from these shores. Finally, the Anglo-Saxons arrived, first as raiders and then as settlers, followed in the 11th century by the Normans.

The pattern of habitation of this landscape is largely one of small hamlets comprising one or more farms, as at Ottinge, with larger market settlements located at Lyminge and Elham. Most of these settlements and farms probably originated in the Iron Age if not earlier. Some buildings survive from these early periods of habitation, notably medieval timber-framed houses at Elham. Buried remains of early settlements dating from the Iron Age onwards and of the cemeteries in which the inhabitants buried their dead, have also survived, some of which have been excavated by archaeologists. As the walk progresses along its route, examples of these surviving remains are indicated and described.

Elham Valley Railway

Although a railway through the Elham valley was first sanctioned as long ago as 1866,

Canterbury city wall

it was not until the late 1880s that trains passed through this quiet backwater. Built by the South Eastern Railway Company (SER), primarily it served as a defensive measure against the rival London, Chatham and Dover Railway whose directors were intent on stealing valuable traffic by opening a line through the Alkham valley from Kearsney to Folkestone. In order to win parliamentary backing, the SER was obliged to engineer the Elham valley line to main line standards with double track. Such high costs could barely be justified at the time, but surprisingly the line did eventually go some way to proving its worth.

Opened in two stages, trains began running between Shorncliffe (near Cheriton) and Barham on 4 July 1887, calling at the intermediate stations of

Lyminge and Elham. Two years later the Canterbury extension was opened when the completed railway was joined up to the Ashford - Ramsgate branch at Harbledown. Three stations were opened on this section, at Bishopsbourne, Bridge and South Canterbury.

Not unexpectedly, the railway had a significant impact on the lives of those who resided along the route, most of whom had been solely dependent upon the horse-drawn vehicle. New markets for local produce suddenly materialized with the arrival of the railway and these opportunities were soon grasped. Livestock, coal, coke, grain, milk, newspapers, machinery and, ironically, road-building materials, were easily transported. All manner of household and commercial wares flowed in, as well as a significant number of visitors

Cottage, Patrixbourne

who came to stay at fashionable Folkestone during the season. The railway also provided a most convenient link between the ancient city and the south coast of Kent, whilst cheap excursion fares enabled many locals, most of whom had rarely strayed beyond their parish boundaries, to sample the delights of the seaside.

Deposits of suitable clay at Exted, near Elham, enabled a flourishing brick-making industry to spring up next to the railway. Puddled clay was piped down from the hills to settling tanks located alongside the kilns where sidings to the north of Elham station were specifically laid down. The SER also opened intermediate sidings at Ottinge and Wingmore for the use of local farms.

During 1897 test borings for coal were made in the vicinity of Lyminge

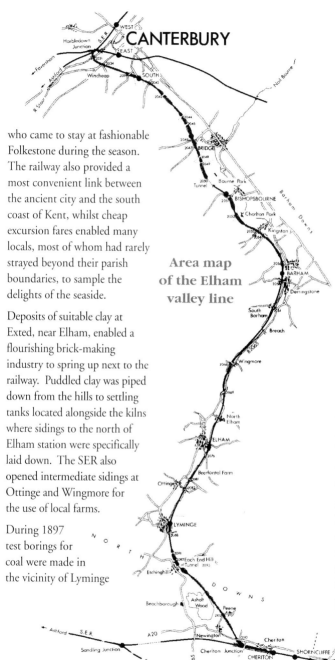

Area map
of the Elham
valley line

and Barham during exploration of the Kent coalfields, but the thin deposits were worthless, otherwise the course of history for both valley and railway would have been quite different.

Until the Great War, the railway enjoyed a virtual monopoly. However, passenger traffic was gradually usurped after 1919 when 'buses began plying the route. Nevertheless, most schoolchildren continued to use the trains, whilst many villagers preferred the railway due to its speed and comfort. Goods traffic saw less of a decline and frequently there were busy spells throughout the year, the most well-known being the annual lamb sale at Lyminge. Quite often as many as 200 wagons were loaded and taken out in what amounted to a very busy day's work for all concerned.

To economise, the railway was reduced to single track north of Lyminge in 1931, but receipts continued to dwindle even though the Elham valley remained popular for Sunday School excursions and with a growing number of ramblers.

Lyminge Station 1927 (by courtesy of Folkestone Library, KCC Arts & Libraries)

Numerous special trains were laid on in a decade when getting out into the countryside was all the rage among suburban dwellers.

With the outbreak of war in 1939 the Southern Railway (SR) handed everything over to the military who not only established defensive gun emplacements at Lyminge and Elham, but stabled a huge rail-mounted howitzer, with an 18 inch ex-naval barrel, on a loop line in Bourne Park tunnel.

Designed as an anti-invasion weapon, it was inspected by Winston Churchill at Bishopsbourne station in 1941, whilst shock waves from its test firings brought down many a ceiling in nearby Barham and Kingston.

After the war the usefulness of the railway had mostly seeped away since villagers were accustomed to using the buses. A trial restoration of passenger services by the SR between

Folkestone and Lyminge failed, and goods receipts were not enough to justify the line's retention, thus complete closure followed in June 1947. All the stations were sold off to become private dwellings, but today only the buildings at Lyminge, Bishopsbourne and Bridge survive. However, other tangible reminders of this lost railway still exist and you will find many remnants along the route. Despite entire stretches

of the trackbed having disappeared under the plough, there remain ivy-covered bridges, culverts, two tunnels, as well as substantial embankments and cuttings which may be seen from the many public footpaths throughout the district. Whilst the line's original purpose may have gone, its path and earthworks provide a valuable habitat for wildlife 🐾

Elham Valley
Walk planning
and preparation
Organisation et préparation
de la randonnée

Walking advice

No season of the year is closed to walkers; enjoyment can be gained from walking on a bright crisp winter's morning, or on an Indian summer's day in the autumn. Equally rewarding is a springtime walk when the countryside is full of new life and growth.

Always wear suitable clothing and footwear for the season. Be prepared for changeable weather. Take with you clothes which are warm and waterproof. Inexpensive overtrousers will protect you from any discomfort caused by walking through high vegetation or crops after rain. Sections of the path may be muddy after periods of rain so wear strong, comfortable and waterproof footwear.

Allow plenty of time to complete your chosen walk. Reckon on walking 2 or $2^{1}/_{2}$ miles (3,2 or 4 km) an hour. The distances and times for each section of the walk are shown on the route maps, and in the information. Allow more time if it has been wet, if you are elderly, or have children or inexperienced walkers with you.

The route has been established in consultation with landowners and farmers and follows public rights of way and permissive paths. Remember that most public paths cross private estates and farmland; some evolved as routes from farms to the nearest village, and were not designed for large numbers of people. Sometimes you are walking through a place of work; enjoy the countryside but please show respect for its life and work. Crops and animals are the farmers' livelihood, and should be left undisturbed.

Always keep to the path to avoid trespass. When faced with a

Straw bales

growing crop you may have to seek a way round the edge of the field even through in law the landowner or farmer is supposed to keep the footpath clear. Walk in single file through a crop. It is useful to carry secateurs to help clear the way if a path has become overgrown. You may remove any obstruction on a right of way sufficiently to allow you to proceed.

Take care when crossing or walking along country roads. Keep to the right, in single file, facing oncoming traffic. On a bend, however, walk on the outside and keep a good lookout for traffic.

Remember to leave things as they are - refasten those gates you find closed. Straying stock can cause damage and an expensive inconvenience to farmers. Always use gates and stiles to negotiate fences and hedges.

Take your litter home with you - it can injure people, animals and wildlife. Guard against all risk of fire, especially in dry weather. Picnicking is not permitted on private land; you only have a right of passage on a right of way.

To avoid injury or distress to farm animals and wildlife, keep your dogs under control at all

times. If not on a lead they can run surprisingly long distances and consequently out of sight of the owner. Please keep dogs on leads, particularly when passing through fruit growing areas or fields with standing crops. Farmers have a right to shoot dogs found worrying animals.

 Conseils aux randonneurs

Portez toujours des vêtements et des chaussures convenant à la saison. Soyez paré contre les intempéries. Emportez des vêtements chauds et imperméables. Un surpantalon vous protègera contre l'inconfort de la marche dans la végétation ou les cultures de haute taille après la pluie. Comme certaines parties du sentier sont boueuses après la pluie, portez des chaussures confortables, robustes et imperméables.

Les distances et les temps de parcours de chaque section de la randonnée sont indiqués sur les cartes d'itinéraires ainsi que dans l'information.

Ne vous écartez pas du sentier afin d'éviter de pénétrer dans des propriétés privées.

Canterbury Cathedral

Using the guidebook

The book is designed to be a practical guide to walking the Elham Valley Way in either direction. It is a guidebook which includes a route guide. It may be used intact or separately by carefully removing the weather resistant route guide from the centre of the book. The guidebook contains a route description, specialist and other information and guidance on planning and preparing for a walk. The route guide, with information about features passed en route, is self-contained and can be used independently of the guidebook.

The route maps have been arranged in sequence in seven sections, from Hythe to

Canterbury. When walking, therefore, from south to north the book is used in the conventional way, whilst the north to south route is read from the back of the book to the front.

By carefully folding it back, the book will fit into a map case, thus providing protection against damage, dirt and damp. Alternatively, the route guide can be folded in half to slip into a pocket when not in use.

Because the countryside is constantly changing, with stiles and gates, and field boundaries being removed or new ones erected, there are no route directions. Route finding should not be a problem given the large scale route maps and the extensive waymarking and signing on the ground.

 Comment se servir du guide

L'ouvrage est conçu pour être un guide pratique de la randonnée sur l'Elham Valley Way, dans les deux sens. Les cartes d'itinéraires ont été placées dans l'ordre, en sept sections allant de Hythe à Canterbury. Ainsi, si l'on marche du sud au nord, on se sert du guide de la façon normale, tandis que pour l'itinéraire nord-sud, on va de la fin de l'ouvrage au début.

Route Options
Options d'itinéraires

The Elham Valley Way is 22^1/$_2$ miles in length and can be undertaken as a long distance walk in one or more days, using the main and/or link routes. A series of circular walks, linked to the main route, cater for the family group or casual walker.

Stile, Newington

 *L'Elham Valley Way s'étend sur 36,8 kilomètres. Il représente une randonnée de longue distance, qui peut être effectuée en un jour ou plusieurs en suivant l'itinéraire principal et/ou ceux de liaison. Une série de randonnées circulaires, reliées à l'itinéraire principal, s'adresse plus particulièrement aux familles et aux randonneurs novices.*

If you wish to undertake the Elham Valley Way in sections you need to be aware of problems of returning to your starting point. Possible solutions might be as follows:

a) Using two cars, one at the starting point and the other at the proposed finishing point;

b) Using one car and public transport. If relying on bus services it is suggested that you make your outward journey by bus thus returning confidently to your car or base;

c) Retracing your steps - the scenery can look surprisingly different when you are walking the other way.

The walk can be undertaken as a whole or in sections, with the suggested following itineraries:

One day

   Hythe to Canterbury:
   22^1/$_2$ miles (36,8 kms), allow 11 hours.

Two days

   Hythe to Palm Tree Public House:
   11^3/$_4$ miles (18,8 kms), allow 6 hours.

   Palm Tree Public House to Canterbury:
   10^3/$_4$ miles (17,2 kms), allow 5^1/$_2$ hours.

Three days

   Hythe to Elham:
   8^3/$_4$ miles (14 kms), allow 4^1/$_2$ hours.

   Elham to Barham:
   6^1/$_2$ miles (10,4 kms), allow 3^1/$_4$ hours.

   Barham to Canterbury:
   8^1/$_2$ miles (13,6 kms), allow 4^1/$_4$ hours.

Four half days

   Hythe to Lyminge:
   6^1/$_2$ miles (10,4 kms), allow 3^1/$_4$ hours.

   (or **Sandling railway station to Lyminge:**
   3^3/$_4$ miles (6 kms), allow 2 hours)

   (or **Cheriton to Lyminge:**
   4^3/$_4$ miles (7,6 kms), allow 2^1/$_2$ hours)

Lyminge to Palm Tree Public House:
5¹/₂ miles (8,8 kms),
allow 2³/₄ hours

Palm Tree Public House to Bridge:
6 miles (9,6 kms),
allow 3 hours

Bridge to Cantebury:
4³/₄ miles (7,6 kms),
allow 2¹/₂ hours.

Alternative routes to Tolsford Hill using the link routes:

from **Hythe:** 5 miles
(8 kms), allow 2¹/₂ hours

from **Sandling railway station:** 2¹/₄ miles (3,6 kms),
allow 1 hour

from **Cheriton:** 3¹/₄ miles
(5,2 kms), allow 1¹/₂ hours

from **Etchinghill:** ¹/₂ mile
(0,8 km), allow ¹/₄ hour

You can devise shorter walks using the bus routes which link with the following places along the route:

Hythe, Sandling railway station, Cheriton, Newington, Etchinghill, Lyminge, Elham, Wingmore, Palm Tree Public House, Barham, Kingston, Bridge, Patrixbourne (infrequent), Barton Estate, Canterbury.

Circular walks

The following circular walks form alternative routes, and link routes along the Elham Valley Way:

① Hythe-Tolsford Hill-Sandling railway station (bus link between Hythe and Sandling):
7 miles (11,2 kms), allow 3¹/₂ hours

② Newington-Peene-Ashley Wood (summer only):
2 miles (3,2 kms), allow 1 hour

③ Etchinghill-Tolsford Hill (take care along busy road):
2 miles (3,2 kms), allow 1 hour

④ Elham Village walk: 1 mile (1,6 kms), allow ¹/₂ hour

⑤ Barham-Derringstone-Heart's Delight-Barham Church (take care on country lanes):
2¹/₂ miles (4 kms), allow 1¹/₄ hours

⑥ Patrixbourne-Bifrons Park: 1¹/₂ miles (2,4 kms), allow ³/₄ hour

Further circular walks are described in the Folkestone, Hythe and Elham Valley Walks pack published by the White Cliffs Countryside Project.

Charlton Park

This page is sponsored by Ordnance Survey

Maps

Cartes

Ordnance Survey sheet numbers and titles.

Titres et numéros des cartes Ordnance Survey.

Landranger Series, scale 1:50,000-1¼ inches to the mile (2 cm to 1 km)

- 179 Canterbury & East Kent area

Explorer Series, scale 1:25 000 - 2½ inches to the mile (4 cm to 1 km)

- 138 Dover Folkestone & Hythe

- 150 Canterbury & the Isle of Thanet

Ordnance Survey maps are available from bookshops, local tourist information centres and post free from Kent County Council, Planning Department, Springfield, Maidstone, Kent ME14 2LX.

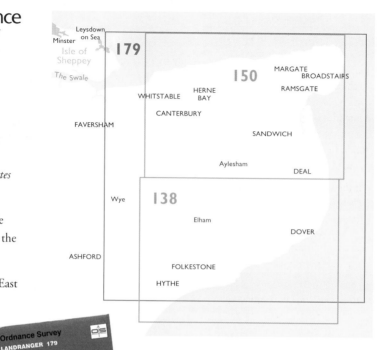

Les cartes Ordnance Survey sont disponibles localement en librairies et auprès des centres d'information touristique.

Grid references

The framework of squares spaced at one kilometre intervals over all Ordnance Survey maps is known as the National Grid. The grid facilitates the pinpointing of any place in the country giving it a unique reference number.

To give a reference number, first take the western (left-hand) edge of the kilometre square in which the place lies. Read the figures at the end of the line in the top and bottom margins of the map, then moving eastwards (to the right) estimate the position of the place in tenths across the square. Secondly, take the southern edge of the same square and read the figures at the end of the line in the side margins of the map. Then, moving northwards, estimate the position of the place in tenths up the square. This gives the place a six-figure reference number accurate to within 100 metres.

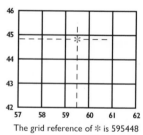

The grid reference of ✳ is 595448

In finding out a grid reference, the first three numbers of the six-figure number refer to the line and number of tenths across the square, whilst the second three numbers refer to the line and number of tenths up the square.

Waymarking and signing

Introduction

The term waymarking refers to marking objects along a public right of way. It complements signposting, which shows where a right of way leaves the metalled road and indicates its initial direction, and enables users to follow a path accurately and confidently at points where they might otherwise have difficulty.

Waymarking benefits not only users of rights of way but also farmers and landowners. It increases users' enjoyment of the countryside and prevents unintentional trespass.

The waymarking system

The recommended system in England and Wales uses small coloured arrows to show the direction of the path and also to act as a target when viewed from a distance. A different colour is used for each category of right of way:

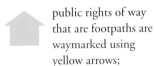 public rights of way that are footpaths are waymarked using yellow arrows;

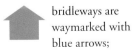 bridleways are waymarked with blue arrows;

 byways open to all traffic and other routes that may legally be used by wheeled vehicles are waymarked with red arrows, but they are intended only to show the status of the route and not to indicate whether it is physically suitable for vehicles.

If the status of a path changes along its length, so does the colour of the waymarking arrows. Where a right of way is part of a special route, such as a National Trail, Recreation Route or circular walk, the arrows are used in conjunction with the route's own symbol.

Elham Valley Way logo

The design of the Elham valley Way logo is an artistic representation of the Elham valley with its church spires which are prominent landmarks along the way.

Transport

Car parking

Car parking places are shown on the route maps. Please note that these are not necessarily car parks. If a car park is not available, please park thoughtfully and sensibly to avoid causing an obstruction or damage to the roadside verges. Leave your car securely locked with valuables out of sight.

Bus and train services

It is not practical to give details of all the bus and train routes and services to, and along the Elham Valley Way, since they may change during the life of this guidebook. Kent County Council publishes an annual public transport map and guide which contains a comprehensive bus and rail route map and a list of bus services and operators (see below).

For details of train services please telephone either (0345) 484950 or London (0171) 928 5100.

You are advised to check details of your journey before travelling, particularly on Sundays. Public transport information countywide can be obtained from Kent County Council, Highways and Transportation Department, Springfield, Maidstone, Kent ME14 2LQ, telephone Maidstone (01622) 696996.

Summerhouse Hill

Transports

Services de bus et de trains

Il n'est pas possible de donner des détails de tous les initéraires et services de bus et de trains reliant l'Elham Valley Way, qui peuvent être modifiés durant la validité de ce guide. Le Kent County Council publie annuellement un guide des transports en commun qui contient un plan complet des itinéraires de bus et de trains ainsi qu'une liste des services et opérateurs de bus (voir ci-dessous).

Pour tous renseignements sur les services de trains, veuillez appeler soit (0345) 484950, soit Londres au (0171) 928 5100.

Il est conseillé de vérifier avant de partir les détails de votre trajet,

House at Elham

notamment pour les services du dimanche. Des renseignements sur les transports en commun dans tout le comté peuvent être obtenus auprès du Kent County Council, Highways and Transportation Department, Springfield, Maidstone, Kent ME14 2LQ, téléphone (01622) 696996.

Useful addresses and/ or telephone numbers

If your have any comments or suggestions about this or any other recreation route, please contact the Access and Recreation Officer, Planning Department, Springfield, Maidstone, Kent ME14 2LX, telephone Maidstone (01622) 696168.

The routes should not be obstructed in any way but if they are please contact the Public Rights of Way Manager, Highways and Transportation Department, Kent County Council, Springfield, Maidstone, Kent ME14 2LQ, telephone Maidstone (01622) 696740.

Tourist information

(including accommodation lists)

Folkestone: Tourist Information Centre, Harbour Street, Folkestone, Kent CT20 1QN, telephone Folkestone (01303) 258594.

Hythe: Tourist Information Centre, Red Lion Square, Hythe, Kent CT21 5AU, telephone Hythe (01303) 267799 (NB not open all year).

Canterbury: Visitor Information Centre, 34 St Margaret's Street, Canterbury, Kent CT1 2TG, telephone Canterbury (01227) 766567.

Walkers' Organisations

Ramblers' Association, 1/5 Wandsworth Road, London SW8 2XX, telephone London (0171) 582 6878

Kent Area Secretary: Mr Peter Skipp, 81 New Street Hill, Bromley, Kent BR1 5BA, telephone London (0181) 857 8571

Long Distance Walkers' Association
Secretary: Mr Les Maple, 21 Upcroft, Windsor, Berkshire SL4 3NH, telephone Windsor (01753) 866685.

Kent Area Secretary: Mr D Sheldrake, 26 Highview, Vigo Village, Meopham, Gravesend, Kent DA13 0RR, telephone Fairseat (01732) 823643.

Youth Hostels Association, Trevelyan House, 8 St Stephens Hill, St Albans, Herts AL1 2DY, telephone St Albans (01727) 855215

Celadine

Conservation Bodies

Kentish Stour Countryside Project, Countryside Management Centre, Coldharbour Farm, Wye, Ashford, Kent TN25 5DB, telephone Wye (01233) 813307

White Cliffs Countryside Project, Countryside Management Centre, Castle Hill, Folkestone, Kent CT19 4AJ, teldephone Folkestone (01303) 274806

Brockhill Country Park, Sandling Road, Saltwood, Hythe, Kent CT21 4HL, telephone Hythe (01303) 266327.

Kent Wildlife Trust, Tyland Barn, Sandling, Maidstone, Kent ME14 3BD, telephone Maidstone (01622) 662012

Countryside Commission, South East Regional Office, 4th

View from Lympne Castle

Floor, 71 Kingsway, London WC2B 6ST, telephone London (0171) 831 3510.

Miscellaneous
Ordnance Survey, Romsey Road, Southampton, Hampshire SO9 4DH, telephone Southampton (01703) 792000

Weatherdial (up-to-date weather forecast) Inland Kent (0898) 14 12 12

Accommodation
Bed and breakfast establishments are located in the following places: Hythe, Saltwood (link route, 1 mile), Cheriton (link route), Newington, Lyminge, Elham, North Elham ($^1/_4$ mile), Barham (link route), Kingston, Bridge, Canterbury. Please contact the Tourist Information Centres (listed on page 22) for details.

For a copy of the Kent Accommodation Guide, contact Kent Tourism, Economic Development Department, Kent County Council, Springfield, Maidstone, Kent ME14 2LL, telephone Maidstone (01622) 696165.

The Ramblers' Association (also listed) publishes the Ramblers' Year Book and Accommodation Guide. The book is available from local bookshops.

Youth Hostel: 54 New Dover Road, Canterbury, Kent CT1 3DT, telephone Canterbury (01227) 462911.

You may join the Youth Hostels Association (also listed) on arrival at the hostel, but prior booking is advisable.

Hébergement
Vous trouverez des Bed and Breakfast aux endroits suivants: Hythe, Saltwood (itin. de liaison, 1,6 km), Cheriton (itin. de liaison), Newington, Lyminge, Elham, North Elham (0,4 km), Barham (itin. de liaison), Kingston, Bridge et Canterbury. Veuillez contacter les centres d'information touristique pour tous renseignements.

Si vous souhaitez un exemplaire du Guide de l'hébergement dans le Kent, contactez Kent Tourism, Economic Development Department, Kent County Council, Springfield, Maidstone, Kent ME14 2LL, téléphone (01622) 696165.

chapter **one**

Seascapes and panoramas

Hythe - Peene

Between Hythe and Peene, the Elham Valley Way contrasts seaside bustle with quiet countryside, and open walks with one of Europe's largest civil engineering projects. From the historic town of Hythe, its High Street colourful with old shop fronts, the Elham Valley Way climbs the old cliff line to a plateau with open views. Northwards, the Way follows tree-arched pathways in old woods and by streams. By stark and dramatic contrast the Way passes the Channel Tunnel terminal, now busy with shuttles taking road vehicles to and from France, freight trains transporting goods and materials and the sleek 'Eurostar' taking passengers to London, Paris and Brussels. North of this massive development, the Way leads through the old settlements of Newington and Peene. Between the two villages, the Elham Valley Way passes by the Elham Valley Line Trust, a community-run museum conjuring up a feeling of the lives of those who lived around the old railway line.

St Leonard's Church, Hythe

Entre Hythe et Peene, l'Elham Valley Way contraste l'animation du bord de la mer avec la sérénité de la campagne, et les longues randonnées avec l'un des plus grands projets de génie civil d'Europe. Depuis la ville historique de Hythe avec sa grand-rue aux vieilles devantures pittoresques, l'Elham Valley Way grimpe la ligne de falaises anciennes jusqu'à un plateau offrant des vues panoramiques. L'itinéraire emprunte, en direction du nord, des chemins sous la voûte des arbres à travers des bois anciens et en bordure de rivières. Par contraste saisissant, le sentier passe près du terminal du tunnel sous la Manche. Au nord de cette impressionnante réalisation, le sentier mène aux sites anciens de Newington et de Peene. Entre ces deux villages, l'Elham Valley Way passe près de l'Elham Valley Line Trust, un musée géré collectivement, qui évoque le mode de vie de ceux qui habitaient près de l'ancienne ligne de chemin de fer.

Fishing boats hauled up on Hythe beach

Hythe

The town and port of Hythe probably dates from the late Saxon period, from the 9th to 10th centuries, and succeeded an even earlier port which formerly existed at west Hythe. From the mid-11th century, during the reign of Edward the Confessor, Hythe was one of the five principal ports which made up the Confederation of Cinque Ports. In return for certain privileges, the Cinque Ports had to provide and maintain ships for the use of the king and for the defence of the realm. The Confederation was a powerful organisation and Hythe flourished between the 11th and 13th centuries.

By the beginning of the 15th century, however, its fortunes were at a low ebb. The town had shrunk to the area around St Leonard's Church, mainly as a consequence of plague but more significantly because of the build-up of shingle in the harbour in the 14th century which rendered it gradually useless as a port.

The town also suffered at least one great fire. The Elizabethan Kentish historian, William Lambarde, writing in about 1570, states that the fire, which took place on 3 May 1400, destroyed 200 houses, and that in the same year five ships and 200 men were lost at sea. It was suggested that Hythe should be abandoned but the king refused to allow this, although the town was relieved of ship service, which it never again provided in full after 1414.

Attempts were made to keep the harbour open and some commercial traffic continued until it too faded. Fishing remained important in the life of the town, as it had done throughout the

Hythe

medieval period, with the Hythe mariners launching their boats from the beaches, a practice which continues to this day. In 1566 it was recorded that 160 of the occupants of the 122 houses in Hythe were engaged in one way or another in this occupation.

Hythe underwent a period of revival in the early 19th century. Due to the fear of invasion by the French during the Napoleonic Wars, a system of coastal defence was constructed between 1804 and 1809. At Hythe this included Martello towers and the Royal Military Canal which begins at Seabrook.

A military barracks was also constructed at Hythe in 1808-09 but finally demolished in 1968. At the height of the wars some 10-15,000 men, both soldiers and labourers, were stationed in the vicinity of the town. The resident population also increased, virtually doubling in the 10 years from 1801-1811, to 2,287.

Despite the end of hostilities in 1815 a military presence was maintained at Hythe closely linked to nearby Shorncliffe. In 1854 a School of Musketry was opened, which later became the Small Arms School, and finally closed in 1968. During the First World War (1914-18), Hythe and Shorncliffe was a major area of training and reinforcement for the British Expeditionary Force. Although there is no longer a military presence in the town itself, gunfire can still be heard from the nearby army ranges ⁊

Hythe lies in a sheltered spot, against a hillside on the sunny Kent coast and is one of the original Cinque Ports. Its Saxon name quite literally means a haven. Well-known for its canal and Martello towers which were constructed to deter Napoleon in the early 1800s, the town boasts a rich tradition associated with the military.

Royal Military Canal and Martello towers

The Royal Military Canal (4) runs across Romney Marsh from Hythe to Pett Level in east Sussex. This was built between 1804 and 1809 to help to defend the rest of England from the much-feared invasion by Napoleon. As a bonus, it was also intended to have practical value in catching water from the higher ground and so relieving flood water on the marsh, as well as providing a means of transport for shingle from the beaches for road making.

There was even a scheme to link the canal with a vast network of canals throughout Kent and open up the interior of Kent to give access to the sea via Canterbury, Chatham, Rye and Hythe. The canal's ability to protect the country from invasion was never put to the test. During the 19th century it provided a useful means of transport. The Environment Agency now controls most of the canal, with Shepway District Council controlling the Hythe section.

The overall line of the canal is north-east/south-west, but you will find it does not run in a straight line. A bend in the alignment occurs every third of mile throughout the canal's entire length. It was designed and built this way so that gun positions could be provided at the end of

Royal Military Canal (County Visuals)

Romney Hythe and Dymchurch Railway (County Visuals)

each length to flank the crossings.

The Martello towers were named after a fort of this type at Cape Martella in Corsica, which successfully repelled a British attack in 1794. Seventy-four towers were built, of which only 26 remain. The tower walls are eight feet thick and built of brick. Round in section, they could only be entered at first floor level by a removable ladder. In two rooms 24 men were garrisoned with their magazine and stores below at ground floor level. The roof supported a cannon on a revolving platform.

Nowadays, Hythe has a reputation for being a clean and healthy resort, popular with visitors who come here to enjoy its picturesque streets, tree-lined walks and promenade seafront. It is also famous for its miniature public steam railway to Dungeness.

Romney, Hythe and Dymchurch Railway

The Romney, Hythe and Dymchurch Railway (1) is the world's smallest public railway line which runs for 14 miles on 15 inch tracks between Hythe and Dungeness. It was the original idea of two racing drivers, Captain J Howey and Count Zborowski. The Count was tragically killed in a motor racing accident in Italy which left the Captain to continue alone with the scheme. The Southern Railway Company eventually offered a site on the Romney Marsh, with a view to expanding their own holiday business. The line was completed and operational by 1929. The miniature steam engines pull a selection of carriages and assorted rolling stock.

Hythe

Whereas most of Hythe's houses date from the 18th century, many medieval buildings survive, whilst Hythe's Norman church fascinates visitors. St Leonard's Church (2) is a parish church of almost cathedral proportions which grew from Norman times with the prosperity of the town. The tower fell down as the result of an earthquake and was rebuilt in the 18th century. Under the east end of the church is a vaulted passageway which containing 2,000 skulls and 8,000 thigh bones. Many stories surround these bones, but it seems likely that they were exhumed from an overcrowded churchyard.

A number of items and memorials in the church and graveyard testify to the strong marine tradition in the town. The memorials include one to Lionel Lukin (1742-1834), a coachmaker who lived in Hythe who became celebrated as the inventor of the lifeboat. Francis Pettit-Smith (1808-1874) is also buried at Hythe. Originally a farmer, he became famous for his invention of the screw propeller for steamships.

Hythe, in earliest times, had a harbour and became a Cinque Port. The title Cinque Port relates to medieval times when these ports provided men and

Skulls, St Leonard's Church (County Visuals)

ships to defend Britain's coasts. In return they received special privileges.

The Town Hall (3) built in 1794 has an imposing white painted portico with a large projecting clock. The ground floor was an open market. Beside this and other buildings in the High Street, run little alley-ways so typical of seafaring communities.

Also in the High Street is the St John's Almshouse. It was originally a leper's hospice and was in existence by 1336. By 1562 it was kept and maintained 'for the needy and poor people and such as were ruined in the wars'. The present building dates from the 16th century and was altered in 1802.

Station Road leads from the eastern end of the town and its name is indicative of an important, but long-forgotten phase in history. When the railway to Folkestone opened in 1843, Hythe had greater status, but persistent petitioning for its own station was not successful until 1874

when a branch opened from Sandling to Sandgate. The new line was intended purely as a first stage in creating a new continental route to Folkestone. Also scheduled for development was the Seabrook Estate, intended to become the 'London-super-Mare' with seaside pier, exclusive residences,

Scene Wood

ornamental parks and squares. Conflicting interests foiled this grand scheme, leaving today's remnants of the railway sole witness to this fruitless dream.

An exhilarating panorama extends from the hilltop

above Hythe with views across Dymchurch Bay, remote Dungeness and beyond to the distant blue Fairlight hills in east Sussex. Looking north and east, you will see St Martin's Plain and Shorncliffe Camp, whilst one of the best views of the entire Folkestone Downs is obtained from here.

Scene Wood

The smooth grass of the golf course stretches between Hythe and Scene Wood; please exercise great care when crossing these fairways. In nearby Paraker Wood there exists a pocket park selected to demonstrate the

importance of woodland management to wildlife. The Elham Valley Way takes you through Scene Wood (5), a very enticing picturesque hollow rich in wildlife. It comprises part of the old Scene or Singe Manor dating back over 900 years.

On the high, broad plains west of Cheriton, the footpath leads across Dibgate Camp (6), established as part of Shorncliffe Camp which dates back to 1784. Generations of young men have camped and undertaken military exercises in these fields. For military, farming and conservation reasons, and also for your safety, it is important that you must stick to the marked public rights of way and must not deviate to get a better view or to try to find something of interest. The area is used frequently and mock battle activity may be seen or heard. Children must be warned not to touch or pick up military debris because of the remote possibility that some may be live.

Primroses

Seabrook valley

The Seabrook valley (7) is named after the small stream which rises at Etchinghill, flows through Ashley Wood and meets the sea between Hythe and Sandgate. Years ago its frequently-swollen and fast-running waters powered corn mills at Newington and Horn Street, but today its course is uninterrupted. Newington Mill was removed to make way for the Channel Tunnel terminal. The stream remains as an important element of the surrounding Site of Special Scientific Interest. A leaflet is available to explain the conservation work being

undertaken here, showing a series of circular walks. For information about these contact the White Cliffs Countryside Project.

Channel Tunnel terminal

An archway carrying the railway to Folkestone, spans the footpath. The bridges which carry the motorway access and the Channel Tunnel rail link (9) leading to the terminal site are awesome and a somewhat dwarfing experience, thankfully these modern structures have been limited to some extent. For example, the bridges have

been restricted to a lower height than the spire of Newington church.

For the time being Channel Tunnel trains will run over the existing main lines from London to Saltwood where the Channel Tunnel link diverges into the terminal. Journey times between London and Paris will be drastically cut in the 21st century with the completion of the independent High Speed Link to London.

Newington

In the tiny village of Newington the contrast could scarcely be greater

between the old world and the new. Indeed, you may well be forgiven for feeling that time has stood still. The history of Newington goes back some 1800 years. Until the 1920s the A20 was a narrow sunken road with high banks on either side, and in the early 15th century it was named Green Street. It was probably first laid out during the Roman period, and was depicted on a late-Roman diagrammatic road map. The Romans stayed

Hythe beach

here for a time, a fact realised when a number of coins and ornaments were unearthed some 200 years ago. William the Conqueror created a manor here and it was recorded as Neventun in Domesday Book.

Detached and untouched, the small Norman Church of St Nicholas (10) with an enlarged chancel, new north aisle of the 13th century and its distinctive spire, seems to stand defiant, surrounded by its lovely old lichen-covered ragstone walls. Among its possessions is a magnificent pulpit dating from the 15th century, here you will also see a curious stained glass window depicting a peculiar and gruesome tale in which St Nicholas is seen resurrecting three young men from a pot. Being the patron saint of the young, among miracles ascribed to him was restoring to life three unfortunate youths who had been murdered and salted down by a wicked innkeeper in whose lodgings they had sought shelter. There is also an unusual brass to

Christopher Reittenger (died 1612), a Hungarian doctor who had been physician to the Tsar of Russia, and other local brasses to members of the Brockman family.

Peene railway museum

Just to the west of the church is Pound Farm (10), named after the pound itself, sturdily constructed in Kentish ragstone with brick capping. It was used to pen straying livestock. Nearby, a little footpath leads westwards towards a quiet hollow known as Frogholt where runs the Seabrook Stream.

Bordering either side of Newington street are small

cottages, one of which reveals that it was once called the Barley Mow (11). This was not a public house, but a beer-house licensed to sell the local brew from Messrs Mackeson of Hythe.

Peene

Peene (20) in its original layout comprises only one farm, now Peene House. The area adjacent to and to the east of Newington and Peene has been subject to a detailed archaeological survey undertaken as a result of the Channel Tunnel Project. Prehistoric, early-Roman and medieval settlements and farms have

been excavated and recorded. The landscape history of the locality has also been studied in great detail from thousands of medieval and later documents.

At Peene you will be able to take a step back in time to an old railway. The Elham Valley Line Trust was established to preserve local railway paraphernalia. There you will see the Trust's collection of former railway buildings and re-created station which houses memorabilia, photographs and historic artifacts associated with the old line. Other items, such as signals, level crossing gates, signs and a full-sized signalbox are laid out with the aim of recapturing the atmosphere of this long-lost railway. A working scale model of the old Elham Valley Railway line is also worth viewing. The museum is open periodically during the year.

During prolonged spells of dry summer weather the walk between Newington and Ashley Wood across the

Pink campions

meadows may be enjoyed. However, at other times of the year the fields are often ploughed and can be heavy-going when muddy, so please be warned. This footpath provides a very different link to Ashley Wood, one of the most important ancient wet woods in the County.

Sandling link route

An alternative start and finish to the Elham Valley Way can be made at Sandling railway station, surrounding which are pleasant wooded slopes and gorse-strewn hillsides.

Sandling station (13) opened in 1888 when it was an important junction with the Hythe and Sandgate branch which, at that period, was expected to be extended through to Folkestone harbour. However, the overgrown trackbed (15) never saw continental travellers and those who are carried on today's main line will eventually use a high speed rail link, leaving Sandling station to slumber.

Brockhill Country Park

Half a mile to the south of Sandling station is Brockhill Country Park (14) which is situated on what was once part of the estate of Brockhill Park. The recorded history of the estate dates back to Norman times. A connection with the death of Thomas à Becket seems likely since his murderers had set out from nearby Saltwood Castle, the seat of 'one of the wickedest men in Christendom', Sir Ranolph de Brock. His name may well have been lent to this estate. Certainly by the time of Edward I, it is known that a Sir Warren de Brockhull was in residence here.

In 1498 the grand-daughter of the last of this line married a John Tournay who took up the estate and it was the last of his successors, a William Tournay who died in 1903 and was buried on the island in the lake.

The owner of Brockhill Park from 1911 to 1942 was Colonel William Tylden, who executors sold the estate to Kent County Council in 1947, when Brockhill Secondary School opened. The country park opened in 1986.

This 54-acre country park is open daily (except Christmas Day) from 9.00am to dusk. It contains the attractive combination of woodland, lake and streams leading to a fine valley from which views of the sea can be obtained.

The footpath north of the railway links the station with Saltwood tunnel (16) where mounds of earth upon its length are indicative of its method of construction. In 1842, navvies toiled for months to hoist huge quantities of spoil out of its vertical ventilation shafts.

Crossing over the M20 bridge and the now-quiet A20 road, a trackway runs between here and the hills, past Bluehouse Wood ❧

Brockhill Country Park (County Visuals)

chapter two

Over the crest
of the Downs

Peene - North Lyminge

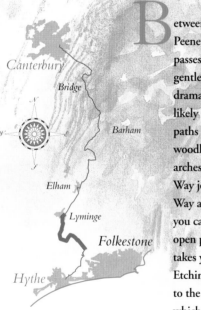

Between North Lyminge and Peene, the Elham Valley Way passes through some of the gentlest scenes and most dramatic panoramas you are likely to find. The route uses paths through ancient woodland and along wooded arches. The Elham Valley Way joins the North Downs Way at Tolsford Hill where you can enjoy the views and open panoramas. A link path takes you to the village of Etchinghill. The route goes to the busy village of Lyminge which has an ancient centre around the church and Tayne Field, with more recent houses centred around the old station.

Entre North Lyminge et Peene, l'Elham Valley Way traverse quelques-uns des plus paisibles paysages et des plus saisissants panoramas que vous pourrez voir. L'itinéraire emprunte des sentiers à travers des bois anciens et des chemins bordés d'arbres. L'Elham Valley Way rejoint le North Downs Way à Tolsford Hill où vous pourrez admirer les beaux paysages s'étendant à perte de vue. Un sentier de liaison mène au village d'Etchinghill.

L'itinéraire rejoint le village animé de Lyminge, au vieux centre s'articulant autour de l'église, puis celui de Tayne Field, dont les maisons, plus récentes, sont rassemblées autour de la vieille gare.

Church of St Mary and St Ethelburga, Lyminge

Summer downland, Arpinge Range

Apple blossom

Folkestone Downs

At Peene a concreted roadway stretches between the road near the bridge abutments and the former trackbed. At this point a good view is obtained of the North Downs escarpment, especially the disused Peene quarry (21) where years of chalk extraction have caused a deep gash in the hillside.

The Folkestone Downs (21) form a dramatic backdrop to Folkestone. They are of national importance for their wildlife and dramatic landscape. Traditional grazing is used to conserve the cowslips, orchids, butterflies and other wildlife. Many ancient tracks cross their heights as well as the Folkestone Downs Walk, developed and promoted by the White Cliffs Countryside Project.

Elham Valley Railway

This section is perhaps the best for walking the old Elham Valley Railway (23) line as it runs for the most part on a dry embankment. Opened in 1889 and closed in 1947, this railway once served the villages and directly connected Canterbury with Folkestone. Along the trackbed you will pass over old bridges which were provided to enable farmers to move their livestock. A valuable wildlife habitat now exists here where the primrose, dog rose, lesser-celandine and cuckoo pint, to name a mere fraction of species, are left to thrive. Hazel, ash, willow and thorn are also in evidence, but try to identify as many species as you can - you may be pleasantly surprised!

Please note that this and much of the land to the east is owned by the Ministry of Defence. Permission has been granted for walkers to use the line of the old railway but you must not stray into the adjoining army training area because of disrupting military exercises, which include the use of blank ammunition and simulated activity or mortar bombardments. Children must be warned not to touch or pick up military debris considering the possibility that some may be live.

Where the alternative route meets the Seabrook Stream (24) a good view is obtained of the embankment and an old railway arch. It is a sobering thought that these entire earthworks were created with little more than spade and barrow, brought

Elham valley railway arch in springtime

from Etchinghill where a deep tunnel was cut through the downs. Excess soil was dumped in nearby Coombe Wood, forming a spoil bank (25) which is easily seen adjacent to the path where a pinetum was planted a century ago.

Ashley Wood

Through Ashley Wood (22), an attractive ancient wet woodland, the Elham Valley Way passes through its beautiful broad-leaved woodland where coppicing is still practised in places. Coppicing allows plants to flourish where a canopy of broad green leaves would otherwise exclude sunlight. Thus careful woodland management ensures proper conservation. The hillside at Coombe Farm provides a useful vantage point to view the formation of the downs.

The North Downs Way and Elham Valley Way combine on the south-eastern side of Etchinghill, skirting thickets of thorn and elder which are valuable native trees for small birds.

Tolsford Hill

From the northern slopes of the deep valley before you, the view southwards extends across to Beachborough Park

Hawthorn blossom at Tolsford Hill

(19) and Summerhouse Hill (17) which rises separately from the main range of downs. Beachborough was once the seat of the Brockman family, but most of the imposing mansion, dating from 1713, was lost in a disastrous fire after the Great War. Across the road

stands the dower house, a most attractive building which has thankfully survived. Less fortunate was the grand hexagonal gazebo

which once stood upon the top of the conical-shaped Summerhouse Hill, a landmark for miles until consumed by fire in 1935 on Guy Fawke's night. Look into the valley below you to see Temple Pond which nowadays is surrounded by trees.

The steep escarpment on which you are standing is one of the highest points in the district. Tolsford Hill (28) is 181 metres high and has been used for grazing for many hundreds of years - look for the well-worn rutted paths. Ancient Britons worshipped here between 3500 and 4000 years ago, and buried their dead in numerous tumuli or sepulchral burial mounds scattered upon its heights. It is not difficult to comprehend why such sites were chosen by our ancestors, given their sense of communion with the sky, earth and elements.

At Tolsford Hill the towering telecommunications mast rises before you. This massive structure beams and receives telecommunications to and from the Continent. Its flashing red light is a beacon for miles around.

Looking north from Tolsford Hill you will catch a glimpse of Elham church spire which, along with others along the

Yellow archangel

valley, was chosen as the Elham Valley Way logo.

The finest views of all are obtained from these breezy slopes where a wide landscape stretches east to west. Folkestone, Cheriton, Hythe, Romney Marsh and the Fire Hills at Hastings (so named due to their proliferation of gorse) spread before you in a scarcely rivalled panorama. Weather permitting, the coastline of France is often visible, whilst Saltwood Castle, the railway viaduct at Folkestone, and Dungeness lighthouse are all enhanced with the aid of binoculars.

Sandling link route

The link route of the Elham Valley Way, running south from Tolsford Hill, follows an ancient hollow lane. This historic landscape feature was formed over many centuries through the passage of farmstock being driven to and from pastures during the seasons.

Crossing the Way at the foot of this steep escarpment beneath Tolsford Hill is the Pilgrims' Way (18) which eventually connects up to Canterbury, from where these old trails radiate across southern England. Many sections still survive as

footpaths or bridleways.

Between Tolsford Hill and the former B2065 road through Etchinghill, there is an opportunity to look along the southern end of the Elham valley from the footpath which passes between cultivated fields and pastureland. Notice how many of the hillsides and surrounding fields are still used for grazing, a tradition that stretches back many centuries in this part of Kent.

Etchinghill

A short link path connects with Etchinghill. The original inn (27) was an alehouse farther down the

road. In the 18th century the landlord purchased two 15th-century cottages, and added on a new wing. He subsequently transferred his business to the more commodious premises, hence the name New Inn. Teddars Leas Road (Tate's Lees) is a byway leading to St Oswald's Church, Paddlesworth where Queen Tate (St Ethelburga) reputedly walked to worship.

Etchinghill was once the home of the Elham Union Workhouse, built in 1835 to house 346 inmates. Opinions differ widely over these notorious Victorian institutions, but on these

Tolsford Hill

premises at least it is related that those who fell on hard times were well clothed, well fed and enjoyed comfortable surroundings. Subsequently the workhouse became St Mary's Hospital. The buildings were demolished in 1997 and the site redeveloped for residential use.

Eighty feet below Teddars Lees Road, a short distance to the north-east of the cross roads in the village centre, and hidden in a tunnel and deep cuttings, runs the trackbed of the Elham valley railway line (26). The excavation here was a considerable feat of endurance by the navvies employed by Thomas Walker who was certainly one of the greatest Victorian civil engineers. The occasional bouts of drunkenness perhaps seem forgiveable when considering the enormity of the task and the back-breaking manual labour that had to be carried out by these men day after day. A hundred years on it seems a piteous waste of human effort and resources where

commercial and financial climates have left it derelict and overgrown. Like many other defunct railway lines, it has become a valuable wildlife habitat.

The East Brook (29) rises near here and forms one of the main tributaries of the Nailbourne, although it is argued that the primary spring bubbles up from a field in Sibton Park. The Etchinghill source was apparently much depleted during the construction of the Elham valley line in 1884 when the deep cutting drained away much of the water into the railway's trackside cess. However, there is often much intermittent water to be seen in the small riverbed, but the local belief that it rises every seven years is not true. For months its course may be dry, then comes a spell of rain when the adjoining fields are sometimes flooded.

Nailbourne legend
Increased demand for water has probably assisted in depleting the natural

underground reservoirs which feed the Nailbourne. At one time local children in Elham used to ride rafts on its waters, whilst one doughty villager reputedly landed a 3 lb trout! The 'Woe Waters' as they were known in the past were superstitiously interpreted as a portender of doom. The most famous legend is associated with the arrival of St Augustine and the Anglo-Saxons' conversion to Christianity. Apparently that period was noted for its dry summers and winters, the land became parched, trees withered, plants wilted and animals died of thirst. Locals who had forsaken their old gods Woden and Thor began questioning the new religion, so the Christian priests offered up prayers for rain. Legend has it that a miracle was performed for, on the spot where St Augustine knelt, a spring gushed forth and a flood of water transformed the Elham valley from a barren wasteland into a verdant landscape once

Poppies

again. However, the old gods fought back and dried the stream, whereupon the Angel of the Bourne descended and renewed its flow. Thus, it is said, the battle rages to this day and explains why some years are dry and others see floods.

St Ethelburga's Well

The pastures between Lyminge and Etchinghill provide a soft springy walk as you follow the Elham Valley Way. Take time to observe the differing landscape features and look out for the attractive pollarded ash trees. Part of this area has recently been developed as a golf course.

Lyminge

At the outskirts of Lyminge (pronounced Limminge), Rectory Lane runs south from the oldest part of the village. Its name is thought to be derived from the river Limen, a watercourse long-since disappeared. There has been settlement at Lyminge at least since the Roman period, and it was also a significant ecclesiastical centre in the Anglo-Saxon period. Archaeological excavations during the 1950s and 1960s uncovered parts of a Jutish or Anglo-Saxon cemetery of the 6th and 7th centuries on the outskirts of Lyminge. During the medieval and early modern periods it was a small rural settlement. In the late 19th century, with the arrival of the railway, it developed as a small agricultural market town due largely to the livestock centre and auction mart held there. This has now become less important and the modern village is largely a residential area.

The Church of St Mary and St Ethelburga (30) is close to the site of the nunnery and monastery founded about 633 AD by St Ethelburga who was the daughter of King Ethelbert of Kent. The church dates from about 965 when it was rebuilt by St Dunstan, Archbishop of Canterbury. It incorporates, in

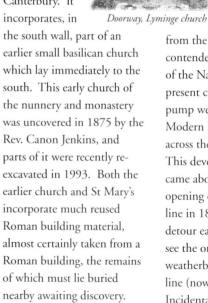

Doorway, Lyminge church

the south wall, part of an earlier small basilican church which lay immediately to the south. This early church of the nunnery and monastery was uncovered in 1875 by the Rev. Canon Jenkins, and parts of it were recently re-excavated in 1993. Both the earlier church and St Mary's incorporate much reused Roman building material, almost certainly taken from a Roman building, the remains of which must lie buried nearby awaiting discovery. The early monastery has the distinction of being the earliest such foundation in England following the re-introduction of Christianity by St Augustine in 597.

Across the road from the church looking east, you will find a quaint well house with a spring gushing forth across Tayne field. This is St Ethelburga's Well (31) and the clear water which spouts from the bank seems a likely contender for the main source of the Nailbourne. The present canopy and chain pump were erected in 1898. Modern Lyminge is seen across the field to the east. This development largely came about soon after the opening of the Elham valley line in 1887 and a short detour east will enable you to see the only surviving weatherboard station on the line (now a County library). Incidentally, those at Elham and Barham were demolished 35 years ago

Summerhouse Hill from Arpinge

High Street, Elham

chapter three
The elusive Nailbourne

North Lyminge - North Elham

At North Lyminge the Way follows the route of the old railway line over old flood meadows, still grazed like the surrounding gentle downs. Between Lyminge and Elham the Elham Valley Way follows the course of the Nailbourne stream which you will see flowing occasionally, only to disappear again except during the wettest winters. The route enables you to visit Elham, a delightful downland village, often regarded as one of the prettiest villages in Kent. It is well worth the few extra steps to enjoy the beautiful church, ancient square with timber-frames buildings and ample supply of village pubs. The Way passes an ancient hamlet just north of Elham with one of the area's oldest farms, now open as a Rural Heritage Centre.

A North Lyminge, le sentier suit le tracé de l'ancienne ligne de chemin de fer à travers de vielles noues, encore pâturées comme les douces collines environnantes. Entre Lyminge et Elham, l'Elham Valley Way suit le cours de la rivière Nailbourne, que l'on voit couler de temps à autre, mais qui est généralement asséchée, sauf lors des hivers très pluvieux. L'itinéraire permet de visiter Elham, charmant village de cette région vallonnée, considéré comme l'un des plus jolis du Kent. Il vaut vraiment la peine de faire quelques pas de plus pour admirer sa belle église, sa vieille place entourée de bâtiments à colombages et ses nombreux pubs typiques. Immédiatement au nord d'Elham, le sentier passe près d'un vieux hameau abritant l'une des plus vieilles fermes de la région, reconvertie aujourd'hui en Centre du patrimoine rural.

Old footpath sign at Ottinge

If you are walking in wet weather you will probably find good quantities of clay stuck firmly to your boots. Infuriating as this is, a thought might be spared for this remarkable asset which, once fired, has for generations given us the building blocks to shelter us from the elements, carried our water, provided the nursery for our plants and seedlings to mention just a few of its uses.

Ottinge

The Elham Valley Way accompanies both the course of the Nailbourne and the old railway between Elham and Lyminge (32) although the route of the latter is sometimes barely discernable, having been ploughed in. Look for old rail posts supporting fences, culverts where the Nailbourne criss-crosses line and ridges in the ploughed fields. An old railway bridge (33) spans the trackbed at Ottinge and carries a quiet lane eastwards, over the hill to Shuttlesfield.

Immediately north of the old bridge was a siding for farmers. Notice the two former railway cottages on the eastern side. Around here you will find evidence of old hedgerows and a fine display of Scots pines. Boyke Manor, nearby, is a

Houses at Elham

restored timber-framed farmhouse originally built by the Lode family in the 15th century.

Walking along the base of the valley the views on either side extend across pastureland which is renowned for producing some of the best sheep in the country. A curious hillock

which you will see alongside the old railway line (34) is marked on old Ordnance Survey maps as an ancient barrow. It is more likely to be a 19th-century spoil heap from a trial pit for coal exploration. A fine southerly view of Elham (pronounced Ee-lum) is obtained from this spot, with the church spire peeping above the trees.

Elham

The derivation of the village's name has always been a matter for argument. Some claim it relates to the number of eels once so plentiful in the Nailbourne centuries ago. Others insist

it is connected with Ula, a former Saxon inhabitant, whilst Domesday records it as Alham.

Although Elham stands a few miles east of the important Roman highway of Stone Street, evidence of their settlement in the village has frequently come to light. Many years ago a silver coin of Hadrian was dug up in the vicarage garden, whilst others were found beneath the church. The Romans were obviously attracted to the valley which supplied them with shelter, fresh water and food. Perhaps the most exciting find was unearthed in a meadow - a beautiful 12th-century brooch with the inscription *Amor Vincit Fortitvdinem* (love overcomes force). Personal and touching items such as these surely reach across the centuries.

Depending on your choice, you may either follow the Way alongside the former railway goods yard, or take the more attractive route through the village.

Elham Valley Way questionnaire

In order to help us assess the success of the Elham Valley Way, we would like to hear your views about the route and the guidebook.

Please would you complete the questionnaire below and send it to the Access and Recreation Officer, Planning Department, Kent County Council, Springfield, Maidstone, Kent ME14 2LX. If you have borrowed this book from a library or friend, you may photocopy the questionnaire.

1. Which of these statements best describes you?

   I live close to the Elham Valley Way ☐

   I came to this area of Kent specifically to walk the Elham Valley Way ☐

   I did not come to this area of Kent specifically to walk the Elham Valley Way ☐

2. Name of town/village where you live *(include post code)*:

   ....

   ....

3. How did you first become aware of the Elham Valley Way?

   Leaflet *(which one)* ☐

   ....

   Word-of-mouth ☐

   Saw sign or waymark ☐

   Advertising *(where)* ☐

   ....

   Newspaper *(which one)* ☐

   ....

   Other *(write in)* ☐

   ....

4. What influenced you to try the Elham Valley Way apart from liking walking?

   ....

   ....

   ....

5. Have you, or do you intend to:

   Walk all of the route in one go, or over a short period of time *(eg. one week)* ☐

   Walk all of the route, in sections, over a longer period of time ☐

   Walk only sections of the route ☐

   Unlikely to walk any part of the route ☐

6. Which of the following modes of travel do you use to get to the start of your walk?

   Walk ☐

   Bus ☐

   Cycle ☐

   Train ☐

   Car ☐

   Other *(write in)* ☐

   ....

7. If you found the walk difficult to follow, what improvements would you like us to make, and where *(please use grid references where possible)*?

   ....

   ....

   ....

8. Please indicate the number of people in each category that accompanied you on your walk *(including you)*.

Age	Male	Female
Under 11	☐	☐
11-16	☐	☐
17-25	☐	☐
26-35	☐	☐
36-45	☐	☐
46-55	☐	☐
56-65	☐	☐
Over 65	☐	☐

Haven't done the walk yet ☐

9. Would you recommend the Elham Valley Way to anyone else?

   Yes ☐

   No ☐

   If you answered "no" please tell us why you say that:

   ....

   ....

10. Where did you obtain this guidebook from?

   Bookshop ☐

   Multiple retailer *(eg. W H Smith)* ☐

   Other shop *(write in type)* ☐

   ....

   Tourist information centre ☐

   Library ☐

   Mail Order ☐

11. What do you like about the guidebook?

....
....
....
....
....
....
....

Is there anything you dislike about the guidebook?

....
....
....
....
....
....
....

12. How useful did you find the detachable route maps?

Easy to read
and understand ☐

Satisfactory ☐

Difficult to follow ☐

Don't know ☐

13. Have you walked any section of these other routes?

North Downs Way ☐

Saxon Shore Way ☐

Greensand Way ☐

Wealdway ☐

Stour Valley Walk ☐

Darent Valley Path ☐

Medway Valley Walk ☐

Eden Valley Walk ☐

High Weald Walk ☐

14. Are you a member of any of the following organisations? *(Please tick boxes)*

Ramblers' Association ☐

National Trust ☐

RSPB ☐

Kent Wildlife Trust ☐

Other walking or countryside organisation(s) *(write in)* ☐

....

15. Are you a regular or irregular reader of any of the following publications for walkers?

The Great Outdoors ☐

Trail ☐

Country Walking ☐

Other *(write in)* ☐

....

16. How do you gain information about walks and events in the countryside?

Local paper ☐

Tourist information centre ☐

Word-of-mouth ☐

Local radio ☐

District/county council ☐

Library ☐

Country park/
visitor centre ☐

Bookshop ☐

Posters/leaflets ☐
(where from)

....

Other *(write in)* ☐

....

17. Are there any other comments you would like to make either about the route or the guidebook?

....
....
....
....
....
....
....
....

18. Having used the Elham Valley Way guidebook, would you consider purchasing Ordnance Survey maps for other walks?

Yes ☐

No ☐

19. Have you, or do you intend to purchase the Landranger and/or Explorer maps associated with this guidebook?

Yes ☐

No ☐

20. Do you own any Explorer maps?

Yes ☐

No ☐

21. I would like to receive more information about waymarked walks in Kent. ☐

I am already listed on the KCC Countryside mailing list. ☐

Tick the box if you would like to receive more information about Ordnance Survey products. ☐

Route map information

Information sur les cartes d'itinéraires

The route maps are reproduced from the Ordnance Survey Pathfinder series enlarged to a scale of 3^1/$_2$ inches to 1 mile (5,5 cm to 1 km). The scale appears on each map spread.

The route maps are arranged in sequence from south to north because it makes following the maps easier. With the north point at the top of each page the maps are aligned the same way you are walking. It is also more comfortable walking northwards since the prevailing wind is behind you from the south-west.

All sections of the Way follow legally defined rights of way unless otherwise indicated on the route maps.

Before using the route guide, walkers are advised to study the key to the route maps and map symbols.

Les cartes d'itinéraires sont reproduites à partir de la Ordnance Survey Pathfinder Series et agrandies à l'échelle de 5,5 cm pour 1 km.

Sur chaque page, les cartes sont alignées nord-sud, et vont du sud au nord au fil du guide. L'échelle figure sur chaque carte.

Distances and times

The distances and times for each section of the route are shown on the map spreads.

The distances in this guidebook are given in miles. The exact conversion of miles to kilometres is 1 mile to 1.6093 km. For convenience the approximate conversion is 1 mile to 1.6 km.

Distance check list

This list will assist you in calculating the distances between places on the Elham Valley Way when checking your progress along the Way.

Route map		Distance from previous location (m)	(km)	Accumulative distance (m)	(km)
1	Hythe	2^1/$_2$	4,0	2^1/$_2$	4,0
2	Peene	4	6,4	6^1/$_2$	10,4
3	North Lyminge	3	4,8	9^1/$_2$	15,2
4	North Elham	3^1/$_2$	5,6	13	20,8
5	Covert Wood	2^3/$_4$	4,4	15^3/$_4$	25,2
6	Kingston	3	4,8	18^3/$_4$	30,0
7	Bifrons Park	3^1/$_2$	5,6	22^1/$_4$	35,6
	Canterbury				

Conversion table

1 mile - 1,6 km
2 miles - 3,2 km
5 miles - 8 km
10 miles - 16,1 km

Waymarking and signing

The Elham Valley Way waymarks are used to show the line of the route in the countryside. You will see them fixed to waymark posts, or posts of gates or stiles. The Way has been waymarked in such a manner that it is possible for you to walk the route in either direction.

The Elham Valley Way logo is incorporated in the different coloured arrows depending on the status of the right of way (see page 21 in the guidebook section). The link routes are waymarked with similar coloured arrows with the words LINK ROUTE printed on the disc.

Changes to the route may occur during the life of this guidebook, in which case look out for the diversion signs and follow the waymarks.

In most places where the Elham Valley Way crosses or leaves a metalled road you will see metal signs fixed to lamp posts or other posts. The logo is added to statutory footpath, bridleway or byway signs, or used on its own where the route follows a section of road.

The Elham Valley Way is not signposted into and out of Canterbury. You are, therefore, given the opportunity of devising your own route to and from the centre of this historic city, to visit the many interesting places and features.

The route is signed to and from St Martins.

Key to route maps and symbols

Key to Ordnance Survey map symbols

Roads and paths

═══════	Motorway
━━━━━━━	Road
━━━━━━━	Other road, drive or track
Unfenced roads and tracks are shown by pecked lines	
··············	Path

Railways

━━━━━━	Multiple track
━━━━━━	Cutting
━━━━━━	Embankment
━━━━━━	Tunnel
━━━━━━	Road over and under
━━━━━━	Level crossing; station

Boundaries

─ · ─ · ─ · ─	County
─ ─ ─ ─ ─	District
··············	Civil Parish

Symbols

▮	Church or Chapel	with tower
●		with spire
+		without tower or spire
▨		Glasshouse
Λ		Beacon
△		Triangulation station
∘ BP, BS		Boundary post/stone
· T, A, R		Telephone: public, AA, RAC
· MP, MS		Mile post/stone
VILLA		Roman antiquity (AD 43 to AD 420)
Castle		Other antiquities
⚓		Site of antiquity
⚔ 1066		Site of battle (with date)

 Gravel pit

Sand pit

 Chalk pit, clay pit or quarry

 Refuse or slag heap

▦▦▦▦▦	Sloping wall
- - - □ - - - pylon pole	Electricity transmission line
∘ W, Spr	Well, spring
[⌗]	Sand, sand & shingle
NT	National Trust

Vegetation

 Coniferous trees

Non-coniferous trees

Coppice

Orchard

 Scrub

Bracken, rough grassland

Heath

Reeds

 Marsh

Saltings

Heights

50 ·   Surface heights are to the nearest metre above mean sea level

Contours not shown

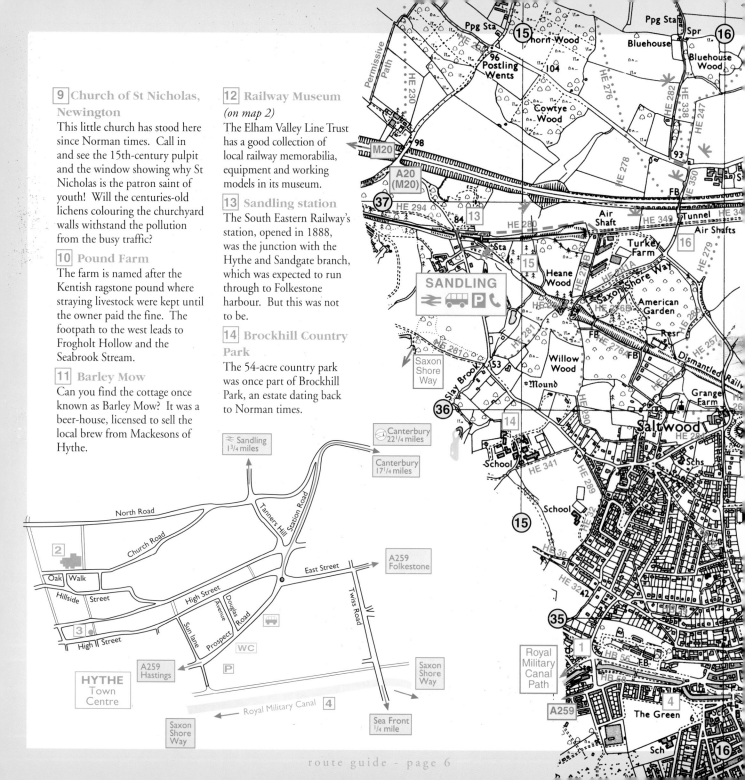

9 Church of St Nicholas, Newington

This little church has stood here since Norman times. Call in and see the 15th-century pulpit and the window showing why St Nicholas is the patron saint of youth! Will the centuries-old lichens colouring the churchyard walls withstand the pollution from the busy traffic?

10 Pound Farm

The farm is named after the Kentish ragstone pound where straying livestock were kept until the owner paid the fine. The footpath to the west leads to Frogholt Hollow and the Seabrook Stream.

11 Barley Mow

Can you find the cottage once known as Barley Mow? It was a beer-house, licensed to sell the local brew from Mackesons of Hythe.

12 Railway Museum

(on map 2)

The Elham Valley Line Trust has a good collection of local railway memorabilia, equipment and working models in its museum.

13 Sandling station

The South Eastern Railway's station, opened in 1888, was the junction with the Hythe and Sandgate branch, which was expected to run through to Folkestone harbour. But this was not to be.

14 Brockhill Country Park

The 54-acre country park was once part of Brockhill Park, an estate dating back to Norman times.

17 Summerhouse Hill

HE 257A

17

HE 259

Sheepfold

HE 257A

HE 258

Truck's Hall W 57

Little Stone Wood

63 FB

Frogholt House

HE 258

HE 259

Works

HE 251

Frogholt

HE 252

Pol

Frogholt Cross Roads

Pilgrims Way Trackway

Spr

18

Peene

19

NEWINGTON

11

10

9

8

!

2

HE 251

Channel Tunnel Exhibition Centre

Channel Tunnel Terminal

M20

CHERITON
all facilities execpt ⊟

37

Cheriton

Bargrove

7

TA Camp

St Martin's Plain

Underhill House

Caldbrook Stream

HF 41

Sch

66

A20
Folkestone
2 miles

The Stadium

Risborough Barracks

Hythe beach

Dibgate Camp

6

HB 11

HB 9

HB 10

7

Casebourne Wood

Casebourne Farm

32

FB

36

19

Dibgate Farm

5

HB 8

1

Scene Wood

HB 13

HB 11

W

HB 12

Plantation

HE 286

HE 285

Sene Farm

HB 8A

HB 14

HB 15

Paraker Wood

HB

Canterbury
17¼ miles

CH

97

HE 287

HB 17

HB 8

Sene Valley Golf Course

Cemy

HB

HB 23

FB

HB 22

Lewty Barn

HB 9

25

!

Sch

Schs

Hospital

A259
Folkestone
3½ miles

35

Seabrook

Royal Military Canal Path

HE

4

HB 58 FB

Golf Course

N

FB

HYTHE
all facilities execpt ⊟

Hotel

0

I Kilometre

I Mile

© Crown Copyright. LA076708

---

15 Dismantled railway
The overgrown trackbed of the disused branch line between Sandling and Hythe.

16 Saltwood tunnel
Compare the method of constructing this 19th-century tunnel with its newer neighbour. The mounds of earth still discernible along its length were laboriously hoisted by hand through the vertical ventilation shafts.

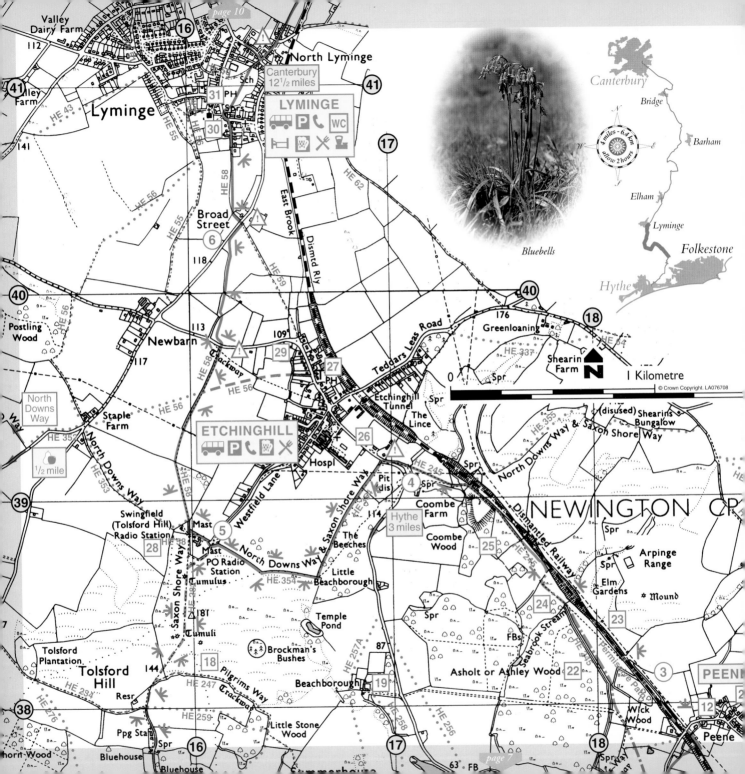

Bluebells

section **two**
Over the crest
of the downs

Peene - North Lyminge

17 Summerhouse Hill
(on map 1)
This conical hill was even more of a landmark until the grand gazebo atop it succumbed to fire on Guy Fawkes night, 1935. Views from the hill include Temple Pond.

18 Pilgrims' Way
Like many other tracks leading eventually to Canterbury, this ancient path is nowadays named for those who journeyed in hope to the shrine of Thomas a Becket.

19 Beachborough Park
The 18th-century mansion, seat of the Brockman family, was completely burnt down soon after the Great War. The attractive dower house across the road survives.

20 Peene
In its original layout, Peene comprised of one farm, now Peene House.

21 Folkestone Downs and Peene quarry
The chalk grassland on Folkestone Downs provides a wealth of wild flowers, insects and birdlife, best in spring and summer. Look especially for cowslips, orchids and butterflies.

The disused Peene quarry is a good access point. You will get excellent views from there.

22 Ashley Wood
Parts of this ancient woodland are still managed by coppicing, to the benefit of wildflowers growing under the trees. You should be able to find evidence of the regularly cut stumps regrowing after the wood is harvested in the traditional way.

23 Disused railway track
The path follows the disused Elham Valley Railway line which once linked Canterbury and Folkestone. The bridges allowed farm stock to pass safely underneath.

24 Seabrook Stream
A small stream which rises at Etchinghill, flows through Ashley Wood and meets the sea between Hythe and Sandgate.

25 Spoil bank
The railway embankment you see from here was built up with spoil from the Etchinghill tunnel to the north-west. The excess soil was dumped, forming a spoil bank.

26 Etchinghill railway tunnel and cutting.
Eighty feet below Etchinghill and hidden in a tunnel and deep cuttings runs the trackbed of the former Elham valley line.

27 New Inn
The New Inn, an 18th-century amalgamation of two 15th-century cottages, replaced an old alehouse further down the road, hence the name. Can you distinguish the 18th-century addition from the original part of the building?

28 Tolsford Hill
At 181 metres, you are standing on one of the highest points of the area. Modern man uses the height for a telecommunication mast to relay signals across the English Channel. Ancient Britons valued such places too; see the burial mounds around you.

29 East Brook
This stream, a major tributary of the Nailbourne, apparently shrank with the construction of the Elham valley line. The deep cuttings are said to have drained off the underground water feeding the spring which is its source.

30 Church of St Mary and St Ethelburga
St Dunstan of Canterbury rebuilt this ancient church in 965. You can still make out part of the even earlier building in the south wall. The early church was part of the nunnery and monastery founded in the 7th century by Ethelburga, daughter of King Ethelbert of Kent.

31 St Ethelburga's Well
This crystal clear spring may well be the main source of the Nailbourne. The canopy and chain pump date from 1898.

Mile

North Downs Way | Saxon Shore Way

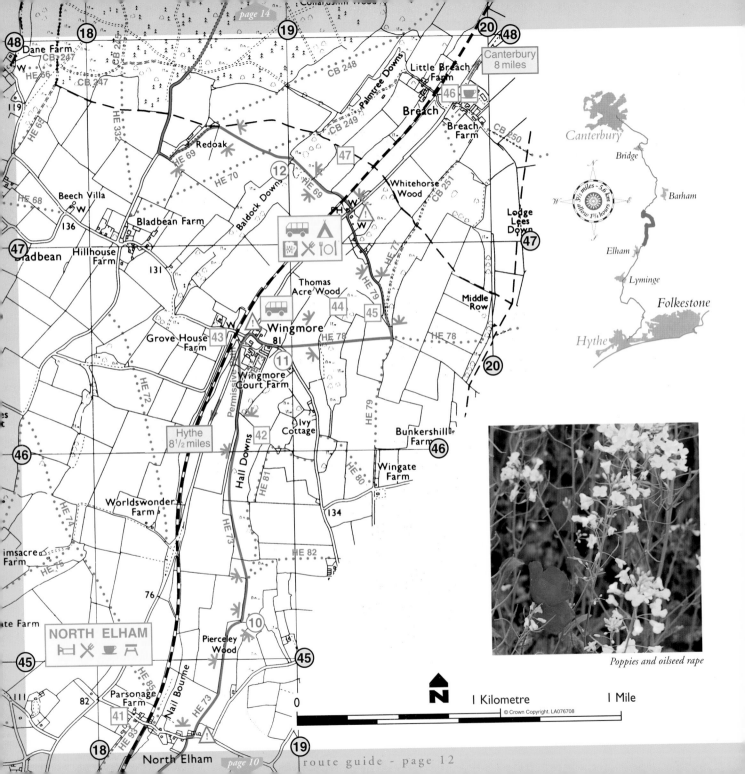

page 14

18 48 Dane Farm
CB 247
W
HE 66
CB 247
119
HE 68
CB 225
HE 332

19

20 48

Canterbury
8 miles

CB 248

Palmtree Downs

Little Breach
Farm

Breach

46 ☕

CB 249

Breach
Farm

CB 250

Redoak
HE 69

Whitehorse
Wood

CB 251

HE 70

12

47

HE 69

Beech Villa
HE 68
W
136

Bladbean Farm

Baldock Downs

PH W
W

Lodge
Lees
Down

47

47

Bladbean

Hillhouse
Farm

131

HE 77

🚌 ⛺
🍇 🍴 🍽️

HE 79

Thomas
Acre Wood

Middle
Row

44
45

🚌

20

HE 78

Wingmore

Grove House
Farm

43 W ⚠️
81

11

HE 78

Thomas Acre Wood

HE 72

Wingmore
Court Farm

HE 79

Ivy
Cottage

Bunkershill
Farm

46

46

Hythe
8½ miles

42

Hall Downs

HE 81

HE 80

Wingate
Farm

HE 74

Worldswonder
Farm

134

HE 82

imsacre
Farm

HE 75

76

HE 73

10

45

Pierceley
Wood

45

NORTH ELHAM
🛏️ 🍴 ☕ 🏕️

HE 85

111

82

Parsonage
Farm

41

HE 73

18

North Elham

19

page 10

route guide - page 12

Canterbury

Bridge

Barham

Elham

Lyminge

Folkestone

Hythe

N
allow 3½ miles - 5.6 km
allow 1¼ hours
W E
S

Poppies and oilseed rape

0   1 Kilometre   1 Mile
N
© Crown Copyright. LA076708

section four
Criss-crossing the valley

North Elham - Covert Wood

41 Rural Heritage Centre
The centre at Parsonage Farm has displays on all facets of rural history. The hedgelaying and coppicing you see along the Way are just two of the rural crafts featured.

42 Hall Downs
The downland here is an excellent example of how appropriately grazed (not too heavily, not too lightly, and at the right times of the year) chalk grassland can produce wildflowers in spring and summer.

43 Wingmore bridge
Looking north, can you make out the bridge over the old railway below you? Yesterday's walkers must have sat here watching the steam trains puffing their way through the landscape, a slight hint of smoke drifting up to join the perfume of the chalk flowers.

44 Thomas Acre Wood
Sights and sounds again in this ancient woodland. Insects, birds, plants - you could even number the different mosses by their different textures.

45 Old hollow lane
Wheels, feet and water have hollowed out this lane over many centuries. The gnarled trunks of some of the hedgerow trees document their age too.

46 Elham Valley Vineyards
Established in 1979, the vineyard has produced award-winning wines. You can sample their wares, by the glass, bottle or cask.

47 Baldock Downs
Contrast this downland with Hall Downs. Lack of grazing lets scrub plants like dogwood and hawthorn take over from the flowers. Some birds and butterflies will appreciate this, others won't. This area, though under-grazed, is by far the better piece of downland and has never been improved.

Different plants appear with the soil change from dry and alkaline chalk to moisture-holding acid clay as the path heads west.

Collie

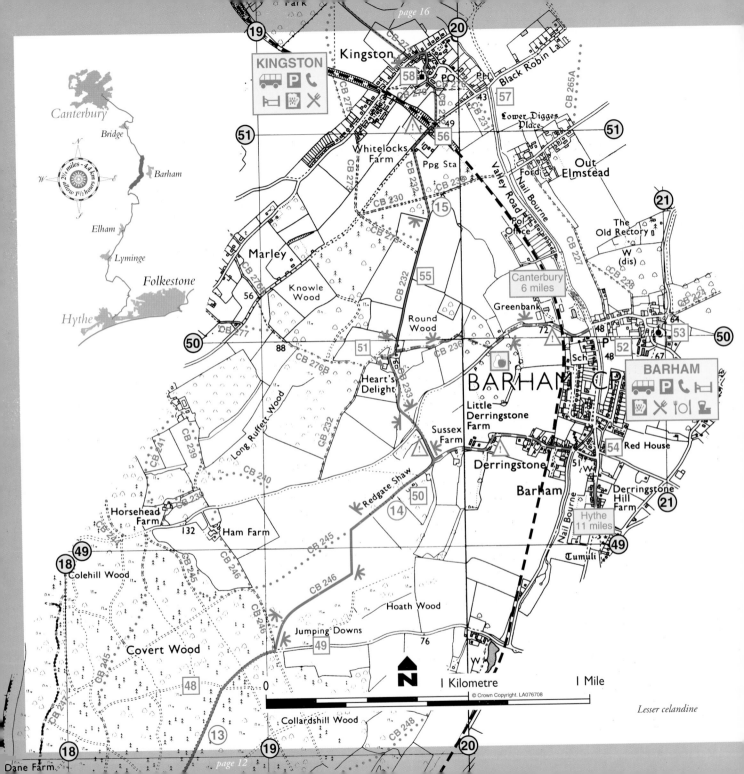

Canterbury

Bridge

Barham

W

Elham

Lyminge

Folkestone

Hythe

2½ miles - 4.4 km
allow 1½ hours

19   20

KINGSTON
🚌 🅿 📞
🛏 ▨ 🍴

Kingston

58   P.O.   P.H.   Black Robin La.

CB 265A
57

Lower Digges
Place

51   51
CB 231

Ford   Out
Elmstead

Whitelocks
Farm   49

56   Ppg Sta

The
Old Rectory

21

W
(dis)

CB 277
CB 230   CB 232   CB 238
CB 279

Nail Bourne P.O.
Office

CB 227

Valley Road

Marley   15

Canterbury
6 miles

CB 228

55   CB 232   Greenbank   CB 224

Knowle
Wood   Round
Wood   72   48   P   64   53

56   50
CB 276   CB 233   CB 236   52   67

88   51   BARHAM C.P.   Sch   48

CB 276B

Heart's
Delight   54   Red House

Long Ruffett Wood   Little
Derringstone
Farm

GB 232   Sussex
Farm   Derringstone   51   W   Derringstone
Hill
Farm

CB 241   CB 239   Barham   21

CB 240   Hythe
11 miles

CB 239   Redgate Shaw   50   49

Horsehead
Farm   14   Tumuli

132   Ham Farm   CB 245

49   CB 246

18   Colehill Wood   CB 245   CB 246

Hoath Wood

76

CB 245   Jumping Downs   49

Covert Wood   W

48

13   © Crown Copyright. LA076708   Lesser celandine

0   1 Kilometre   1 Mile

N

Collardshill Wood   CB 248

18   19   20
page 12

Dane Farm

CB 247

BARHAM
🚌 🅿 📞 🛏
▨ 🍴 🍴 🛍

section five
Along hidden byways

Covert Wood - Kingston

48 Covert Wood

Conifer and sweet chestnut have replaced many of the native trees in this 184-hectare (455-acres) wood. The difference in the number of flowering plants under the shady conifers with the wealth under the native trees is noticeable.

You may hear the drumming call of a woodpecker; each of the three species resident here ratatats on hollow trees at a different rate.

49 Jumping Down

Excellent views towards Barham from here. Skylarks frequent these fields in spring and summer.

50 Redgate Shaw

Shaw is a very early word for a small wood like this, indicating a very long existence. The number of different trees is another indicator of age - how many can you distinguish?

51 Heart's Delight

Heart's Grief once stood near to Heart's Delight! The farmhouse is Tudor, the redundant oasthouse now a private house.

52 Barham

Two highlights of the Second World War for Barham were the crash of a German aircraft on the railway line near this bridge (the crew were captured by the Home Guard) and the visit to the Women's Institute by the wives of Winston Churchill and President Roosevelt.

The village school has an unusual Gothic bell tower.

53 Church of St John the Baptist

The St George window in the 13th-century church is a memorial to soldiers who camped nearby during the Great War.

Nearby is Barham Court. Local disputes used to be settled in the annual manorial courts there. One wing of the house is original 17th century; the rest was rebuilt in 1735 and enlarged by Lutyens in 1911.

54 Derringstone

Infilling with houses has merged Barham with the once-separate hamlet of Derringstone. Don't look for heathland near Heathfield Way - Station Road was renamed after the last and much-loved station porter, Jack Heathfield.

55 Old hedge

Have you ever tried to tell the age of a hedge? Count the different types of tree or shrub in a 30-metre stretch of this very old one; each species adds a 100 years.

56 Railway arch

The stretch of trackbed from above this beautifully constructed arch to Bishopsbourne is a Site of Nature Conservation Interest. Plants include carline thistle, cowslip and hairy violet. On an evening visit, you may see glow-worms and bats.

57 Black Robin

'Rigden Dellman ales are sold Where once did live Black Robin bold'

An earlier sign on the Black Robin Inn referred to a notorious 18th-century highwayman.

58 Kingston church

St Giles Church dates from Saxon times. The wall paintings, font and pulpit are of particular interest.

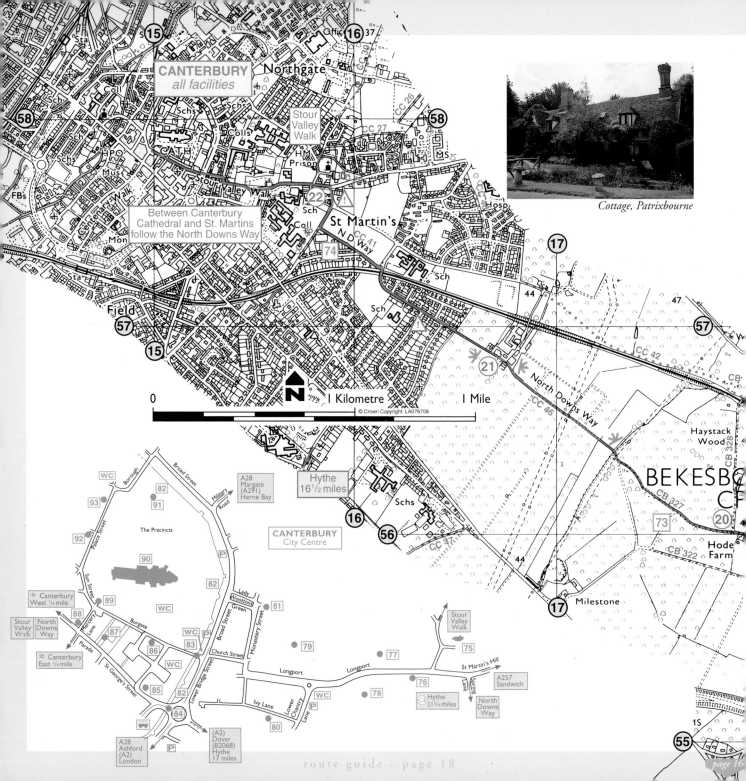

CANTERBURY
all facilities

Northgate

Office

15

16 37

CC 30

CC 26

Stour Valley Walk

58

CC 27

CC 41

58

HM Prison

Stour Valley Walk

Between Canterbury Cathedral and St. Martins follow the North Downs Way

St Martin's

N D Way

22

74

Sch

Coll

Cottage, Patrixbourne

17

44

47

57

57

CC 42

Field

North Downs Way

57

15

21

CC 46

0   1 Kilometre   1 Mile

© Crown Copyright. LA076708

CB 328

Haystack Wood

BEKESBO CF

Hythe
16½ miles

16

CB 327

WC

82

Broad Street

Borough

Military Road

A28 Margate (A291) Herne Bay

CANTERBURY
City Centre

56

20

73

93

91

CC 47

CB 322

Hode Farm

92

The Precincts

Palace Street

44

P

90

82

Milestone

17

Sun Street

89

Canterbury West ¼ mile

88

Lady Wootton's Green

81

Stour Valley Walk

Stour Valley Walk

North Downs Way

87

Burgate

Mercery Lane

WC

P

83

Church Street

79

77

75

Canterbury East ¼ mile

86

Broad Street

Monastery Street

WC

St George's Street

Parade

82

WC

St Martin's Hill

Longport

Longport

76

A257 Sandwich

Lower Bridge Street

85

84

Ivy Lane

Lower Chantry Lane

WC

P

78

Hythe 21¾ miles

North Downs Way

A28 Ashford (A2) London

80

A2 Dover (B2068) Hythe 17 miles

55

1S

The road which crosses the old railway south of the village is known locally as Lickpot Lane, a far more interesting name that its official title, Vicarage Lane.

Delightfully-named Duck Street used to join The Square with the railway station, but except for the old platform facings little else remains. The hillside over to the south-east still bears the scar of the chalkpit where lime was extracted years ago for building purposes. This pit remains a traditional playground for many generations of Elham youngsters who roamed these quiet hills and meadows in an age when life was certainly far more simple and uncomplicated.

In times past Elham was the most important settlement in the valley and once a village with a flourishing market. It retains a genuine old-world feel with its many characteristic buildings and inns which are well worth visiting.

The High Street broadens out almost to a square, and on the western side you will see one of its oldest

St Mary's Church, Elham

buildings, the Abbot's Fireside (33), which is a Tudor building dating from 1614. There are fine carved

brackets to the front elevation and inside there is a fascinating fire surround which was carved by monks

in pre-reformation times, hence the hotel's name. Later, with the threat of invasion by Napoleon, the

'Iron' Duke of Wellington, is reputed to have established an headquarters here while marshalling his troops.

Opposite, stands the Rose and Crown (36), at one time a staging post for horse-drawn coaches. This old inn still retains a large yard and stables. It also has upstairs rooms which were used for a fortnightly magistrates' court.

Eastwards, St Mary's Road connects into The Square (37) which probably has its origins in the 13th century following the Charter of 1251 granted by Prince Edward. Around three sides it is bordered with buildings of varying antiquity, for example, King Post (38) on the northern side, now owned by the National Trust, has a Georgian frontage, but the remainder of this fine medieval hall house has a wealth of old beams.

South of The Square, a row of cottages stood until 1942, but now the view to the church (30) is uninterrupted. Notice the ancient flint walls of the churchyard which are home to ferns, valerian, ivy and the ever-wandering toadflax. The original church, mentioned in Domesday, disappeared but the present Early English structure built about 1200 and dedicated to St Mary is delightful both inside and out. The fine western tower and spire were added in the 14th century, followed by further rebuilding in the 15th century when the nave was heightened and given a clerestory. Of interest inside is a 15th-century stained glass window depicting Thomas à Becket, a 700-year-old crusader yew chest hewn from a solid log, and an unusual altar dedication to St Catherine, the patron saint of spinsters.

Elham once possessed two windmills, the larger standing high above the village on the western hillside, whilst the post mill on Elham Down was lost in a storm a century ago.

Wooden cottage at Elham

Elham

Numerous prehistoric and Roman artifacts have been found at various locations within the parish, and it is likely that, like Lyminge, it was an important place during the Roman period. The sites of some former earthen burial mounds now levelled by ploughing are known from air photographs. In its present form and layout Elham represents a small medieval town composed of a group of farms to which have been added modern residential houses. Its main interest lies in its timber-framed buildings several of which are still standing. There are also a number of subsidiary settlements such as Ottinge. There are also several medieval and post-medieval landscape features remaining which reminds us of how the countryside was both managed and exploited during former times.

At the site of the old level crossing (40) (notice the hump in the road) the Way follows the route of the railway, but its course is barely detectable. Should you stumble across a brick you might find it stamped EVC for it was here, on the eastern side, that the Elham Valley Company had its kilns. Many of these bricks were used for local houses, whilst the railway likewise bought them for bridge construction along the line during 1885.

The Nailbourne flowed too infrequently to be relied upon as a source of fresh water, supplies of which were found through the sinking of wells and pumps. Some Elham houses had their own well, such as King Post in The Square, whilst communal wells were often sunk to cater for the needs of a whole group of houses. Although almost all have either been boarded over and disused for many years or filled in, residents who remember using such sources speak highly of the water quality ❧

View looking towards Elham

Elham
Celebrating
the place

As you walk the Elham Valley Way you would be well advised to plan a stop in the village of Elham. There are three excellent pubs to refresh even the most weary walker, several village shops, a restaurant and public toilets. If you plan to take two days to walk the Elham Valley Way you will find Elham an excellent place to break your journey. There are several places offering overnight accommodation in and just outside the village. (please see page 23 for full details).

As you rest in this peaceful and attractive village take a while to look around. Elham is a living, working village where there is a quite justifiable pride in place.

Elham has a classic mix of life-long village people together with those who have moved in to enjoy the attractive surroundings and village life. This mix gives life and energy to the village, a

Mary's Seat

Elham Parish Map

fact which was clearly demonstrated in a recent project designed to record and protect what local people felt was important about their parish.

Poppies

A local group, called the Elham Circle, worked along with the White Cliffs Countryside Project, a local ecologist and the artist, Graham Clarke, to produce a parish map, a record of what local people hold dear. The Elham Parish Map struck a chord, the original map is displayed in the village hall and now you will find prints of it above the fireplace in many village houses. Hundreds of copies have been sold, the income helping to fund a new village hall.

Caring for the place

The Elham chalk pit is a favourite feature of the parish and still a playground for village children. There is a cherished view-point just above the chalk pit, which is the scene reproduced in the Parish Map.

Perhaps rather surprisingly, the chalk pit is also an oasis for wildlife. Much of the downland of the Elham valley has been improved that is, either ploughed and sown with grasses or fertilised; the original flower-rich downland is now all but gone from the valley. Around the chalk pit and along the nearby road verges, ancient unimproved downland remains. As part of the project local people visited the chalk pit to count and record the wild flowers. They found nearly 100 species of wild flowers including four types of orchid and several butterflies as well.

This wonderful but tiny wildlife haven was under threat from trees and scrub that, without grazing, were invading the grassland. Local people now manage the site and with permission from the farmer, Peter Vincent. Trees have been cut back, the grass is cut by hand and raked off to allow the finer wild flowers to come through and thrive. To celebrate this place the Elham Circle has produced a poster of the chalk pit, its flowers and fossils, along with a panel which has been erected in the chalk pit itself.

Discover a little more for yourself

While you're in Elham, why not take a short walk to visit the chalk pit and enjoy the view; go through The Square, past the church and along Duck Lane. You will then follow a wonderful hollow lane with ancient hedgerows on either side of your way. Follow the lane as it climbs and turns to the left and you will shortly be at the chalk pit. Look on the road verge on your left where in May and June you will find masses of wild flowers, and even wild orchids, please don't pick any though. Follow the lane just a little bit further and you'll find Mary's Seat, the latest Elham Circle project, carved by local people with the help of a sculptor, William Glanfield. Rest a while here and take in the wonderful view of the valley before you return to Elham and carry on the Elham Valley Way.

If you want a copy of the Parish Map or chalk pit paintings, they are available

Carving Mary's seat

from several village shops as posters or cards. Separate circular walks cards are also available from village shops.

The work in Elham was part funded by the Kent Rural Action Programme. Contact the Kent Rural Community Council or a local countryside project if you want to do a similar thing for your place ❧

chapter **four**
Criss-crossing the valley

North Elham - Covert Wood

T he Way criss-crosses from one side of the valley to the other, climbing downland banks, through woodland and past old hamlets. Here you will discover hidden and wonderful glimpses of an ancient landscape full of detail and meaning. Above the Palm Tree Public House are chalk banks, arable lands, and woodland plantations of pines and fir.

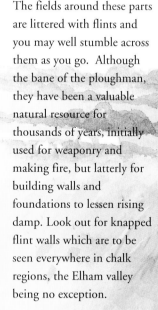

Le sentier zigzague d'un côté de la vallée à l'autre, grimpant des escarpements, traversant des bois et passant près de vieux hameaux. Ici, vous découvrirez au détour du sentier de merveilleuses vues d'un paysage ancien, riche de détails et de sens. Au-delà du pub Palm Tree se trouvent des talus crayeux, des terres arables et des plantations de pins et de sapins.

The fields around these parts are littered with flints and you may well stumble across them as you go. Although the bane of the ploughman, they have been a valuable natural resource for thousands of years, initially used for weaponry and making fire, but latterly for building walls and foundations to lessen rising damp. Look out for knapped flint walls which are to be seen everywhere in chalk regions, the Elham valley being no exception.

When the old wall around Elham church became so dilapidated in the late 19th century, a plea for flints by the Rev. Wodehouse was eagerly answered by

Houses at North Elham

High summer overlooking Elham

surrounding farmers who brought them along by the cartful.

You will likely notice grazing sheep throughout the year in these parts. Sheep stealing was dealt with harshly, with no mercy shown to those found guilty and sent to the gallows. A rather charming piece of Elham folklore speaks fondly of a destitute 14 year-old boy who was convicted of this crime. Flung into the local gaol, the villagers were fearful of the poor lad's appointment with the hangman, so they plied the policeman with drink, before unlocking the cell and hiding the youngster with two elderly village women for half a year. Legend says he successfully made his escape, sailing to Australia where he became a famous sheep breeder.

North Elham

North Elham is an ancient settlement dating back to pagan times, its roots lying in farming.

At Parsonage Farm (41), whose farmhouse has a Norman undercroft and chalk-block walls two feel thick, there is a Rural

Tractor and granary, Parsonage Farm

Heritage Centre. There are displays on all facets of rural history. Many of the old crafts may still be seen along the route, for example the ancient art of hedge-laying is still practised locally.

Perhaps surprisingly, North Elham has long been a separate, distinct settlement, with roots deep in the past. Here, there is a farm called 'Grimsacre' which is thought to denote a shrine established by Jutish settlers who worshipped Woden, known also as Grim.

Hall Downs

The landscape near Hall Downs (42) is certainly one to be enjoyed. It is an important area of chalk downland which offers rich grazing as well as supporting a variety

of interdependent species. Notice how the spire of Elham church rests harmoniously amid the village rooftops and these soft, gentle folds of the hills. Below, and to the north, an old bridge at Wingmore (43) serves as a reminder of the railway and the trains which once trailed clouds of dissipating white steam behind them.

Walking through ancient Thomas Acre Wood (44) there is an opportunity to sample the sights, sounds and smells of this secluded part of Kent. As you walk through here, notice the variety of trees, woodland mosses and plants which support insets, birds and animals.

An extant hollow lane (45) of some considerable antiquity runs between the fields, giving shelter and a chance to ponder upon its great age. Here you will see knotted and gnarled trunks amongst the wayside hedges which have grown here for many centuries.

The Elham Valley Way crosses the route of the old railway and the Nailbourne as you walk down and then climb up the opposite hillside. Do not be surprised if you find the bourne flowing quite fast at this point as it is well fed by surface water which percolates down through the chalk.

To the north-east is the hamlet of Breach where, in 1979, the Elham Valley Vineyards (46) were established. During preparation work Neolithic flint scrapes were unearthed, some dating back 3,500 years before Christ. The vineyard has won medals in the English Wine of the Year Competition and tastings are available. Wine is on sale by the glass, bottle or cask. There is a tearoom also.

Baldock Downs

Baldock Downs (47), on the western slope, are an example of good chalk grassland, although many areas are gradually returning to scrubland due to lack of grazing. Common scrub species such as dogwood, hawthorn and ash are already encroaching and replacing the wild thyme, marjoram, violets, knapweed and salad burnet. West of these downs, acid capping clay soil is suitable for crops which would otherwise perish on downland where the subsoil is very thin, dry and alkaline ❧

Landscape at Wingmore

Bridleway through Redgate Shaw, Derringstone

chapter **five**
Along hidden byways

Covert Wood - Kingston

Covert Wood is a large area of woodland, very much representative of the agriculturally poor, clay topped Kent Downs. Native broadleaves such as hornbeam, ash, oak and hazel have been replaced with sweet chestnut coppice, and in the last fifty years with fast growing conifers. Compartments of deciduous trees along with glades, rides, and trackways still exist, with their associated plants and animals, many of which are attractive and uncommon. The remaining small woods, arable fields, and grazing pastures of this section are typical of the Kent Downs today. The settlements of Barham and Kingston both have ancient churches, and are connected by the fickle Nailbourne and the disused railway line with its old brick arches.

Covert Wood est une vaste zone boisée, tout à fait caractéristique des Kent Downs, ces collines argileuses faiblement cultivées. Les feuillus indigènes tels le charme, le frêne, le chêne et le noisetier ont été remplacés par des taillis de châtaigniers, et ces cinquante dernières années par des conifères à feuilles caduques, comportant clairières, pistes cavalières et sentiers où vivent divers animaux et plantes, dont beaucoup sont beaux et rares. Les petits bois, les terres arables et les pâtures qui restent dans cette section sont typiques des Kent Downs aujourd'hui. Les villages de Barham et de Kingston, qui possèdent chacun des églises anciennes, sont reliés par la capricieuse rivière Nailbourne et la ligne de chemin de fer désaffectée aux vieilles arches en brique.

Stained glass window in St Giles Church, Kingston

Canterbury

Bridge

Barham

Elham

Lyminge

Folkestone

Hythe

Covert Wood

Covert Wood (48) is 184 hectares (455 acres) in extent, with the majority owned by the Forestry Commission since 1925. Douglas fir and beech, along with coppiced sweet chestnut are now the three most abundant species of tree, but originally most species here comprised coppiced hazel, hornbeam and ash with standards of oak.

Douglas fir given the right conditions can grow to be the second tallest tree in the country, after the redwoods. However on shallow soils it is prone to disease and may be blown down easily. It can provide very fine timber used in building, doors, floors, veneers and high quality ply. To identify it look for the two bands on the underside of its leaf. The other conifers along the road are western hemlock and European larch.

Unfortunately the dense shade created by conifers excludes growth on the woodland floor, however, glades and trackways and areas which are still deciduous in nature enable both rare and common native plants to flourish. Along the road in spring lookout for celandine, wood anemone, primrose, yellow archangel, bluebells, wild garlic, moschatel and wood sorrel whilst ground ivy, wood sage, bush vetch, great wood rush, scabious and

Chestnuts

black knapweed can be seen throughout the summer. All of these plants make the most of the dappled sunlight which percolates through the greenwood canopy and the earlier ones take advantage of the light before leaves come onto the beech and coppice trees. Deeper in its depths a variety of orchids exist, whilst ancient woodland indicator plants of which there are over 70 species including butcher's broom, woodruff and herb paris suggest that its history probably dates back at least to the middle ages. Covert Wood is also valuable to birds, among its residents are nightingales, hawfinches, tawny owls and three species of woodpecker.

By looking carefully along either side of the road in the autumn you might see a wide variety of fungi including some of the following: the blusher, honey fungus, candlesnuff fungus, shaggy parasol, brown roll rim, magpie fungus and fly agaric.

Despite the wood's commercial value and activity, it retains many important conservation pockets.

If you would like to explore the wood further there are circular waymarked trails. One of which leads off from the road along an ancient wood bank and is marked by a post painted on the top with a white badger paw print.

The hornbeam tree illustrated on page 78 and 79 is this shape because it has at some stage in its life been layed. This is the process of cutting boundary trees and bushes down to form a thick living barrier. There are many hornbeams similar to this along the boundaries of Covert Wood.

Jumping Downs

At Jumping Downs (49) there are good views to Barham, although the Black Mill which once stood as a landmark for miles upon its windswept ridge was lost in a fire during restoration 25 years ago. In this vicinity there exists today a motorcycle circuit, but hopefully the only sound to greet your ears will be the skylarks which frequent these fields at times of the year.

The bridleway which forms the Elham Valley Way through Redgate Shaw (50) is annually bordered with common springtime flowers, whilst a surprisingly wide variety of trees can be found. The word shaw is Kentish terminology, originating from Scandinavia, for a small wood or copse. Almost every one of these Kentish shaws pre-dates the Saxon period when they were vital for supplying timber for building, cooking and heating. Many shaws exist throughout this district, providing valuable retreats for wildlife. You should be able to pick out ash, field maple, chestnut, hornbeam, cherry, oak, sycamore, hawthorn, holly and guelder rose, but try and see how many trees and shrubs you can count.

Heart's Delight

North of Old Scratch Shaw lies Heart's Delight (51) where the way leads past a homestead and a small pond. Hops were once grown on the farm but the oasthouse has

long been converted into a residence. The old farmhouse dates from Tudor times but its cellars are claimed to provide evidence of an earlier, monastic, building on this site which was used by the lay priests of Canterbury. Another house, known curiously as Heart's Grief once stood nearby but was lost in a fire many years ago.

Barham link route

The hill-top orchards to the east through which one of the link paths to Barham leads, provide a wonderful northwards view to Kingston and a glimpse of the Barham Downs which have been the site of many battles. During the Roman invasion the Britons fought hard to repel

Caesar, but fell beneath the conquering hoards who left no man alive on these slopes. Celts, Romans, Britons and Saxons have all battled here, whilst the four-mile range is littered throughout with ancient earthworks and tumuli.

Near the bottom of Green Hills are the abutments of the old railway bridge (52). A German Dornier crashed on the line here in 1940, but the crew emerged unscathed and surrendered to the local Home Guard. During the Second World War Mrs Roosevelt, wife of the American president, and Mrs Churchill travelled by special train to Barham to visit the local Women's Institute.

Throughout these dark days the skies above the Elham valley were the backdrop to many 'dogfights' when this part of Kent justly earned the title Hellfire Corner.

Barham

Barham dates from Saxon times (ham means a settlement). At the main road in Barham you will see the village school (52) with its distinctive Gothic bell tower, whilst across the road to the east lies the old village of Barham (pronounced Barrum to rhyme with Baron). Set upon the eastern side of the valley, it nestles around the church (53) which sits majestically among the trees. Dedicated to St John the Baptist, it was built during

Bowling at Barham

the 13th and 14th centuries. It possesses many fine artifacts, including a beautiful window depicting St George slaying the dragon. This was presented by the survivors of the 23rd Signal Company RE as a memorial to their lost comrades who camped in the surrounding fields during the Great War.

Near the church is Barham Court which was originally the court lodge of the manor of Barham before it became united with Bishopsbourne and where the manorial courts were held annually. These courts held jurisdiction over local matters, including keeping the peace, at a time when the parish was for most people the focus of their lives. The main part of the present house was rebuilt in 1735 but a surviving wing is of the 1600s. It was enlarged and refurbished by Sir Edwin Lutyens for Evelyn Stanton in 1911.

Derringstone

Derringstone (54), which lies to the south, once existed as a hamlet quite separate from

Hedgeparsley

Barham, but sporadic housing developments have caused these places to merge. Heathfield Way used to be called Station Road for obvious reasons, but was renamed in honour of its last station porter Jack Heathfield who was very much a colourful and well-loved local character. Very little remains of the old line today, but Barham still possesses a road called Railway Hill, at the bottom of which you will periodically find the Nailbourne flowing across the ford.

A hundred years ago you would have been able to watch the magnificent horse-drawn coaches which plied the Elham valley road

between Folkestone and Canterbury. The coaching era came to a close during the 1890s, killed off by the superior service offered by the new railway. One of the most famous was the Sporting Times driven by Mr James Scott, but he met a sad end in 1896 when his coach hit a tree stump at the foot of Derringstone Hill, overturned and caused him terrible injuries. Poor Scotty was carried to the Red House nearby, but sadly he never recovered and the great age of the coach in these parts died with him.

The soil in the vicinity of Breach and Barham supports grazing and chief crops such as oats, barley, wheat and peas. The clay is good for firing and, not surprisingly, a brick and tile works once existed here, whilst occasional acts of demolition still reveal bricks stamped BARHAM. However, nothing could be more pleasing than to see how the local clay has provided building materials which blend so

harmoniously with their surroundings. The rust-red hues of the roofs contrast exquisitely with the greenery of the surrounding trees, and create an effect that is quite unobtainable in these dreary days of mass production.

Old hedge

The lane which leads to Heart's Delight (55) shows evidence of very great age and whilst walking you might try counting the variety of hedgerow species. Among those more easily identifiable are blackthorn, wayfaring tree, dog rose, spindle, holly, elder, field maple, wild cherry, ash, holly and yew, all of which provide a varied food supply for wildlife. According to Hooper's Law (an Oxford professor who studied hedges for many

Dog rose

years) one species found in a hedge, in a random 30-metre section, is equivalent to a 100 years. Whilst this does not take into account that many hedgerows today are planted as multi-species, it is, nonetheless, a handy guide when out walking the many paths and lanes in the countryside.

Near Kingston, the Elham Valley Way passes beneath a substantial brick railway arch (56). The trackbed above has become a Site of Nature Conservation Interest and stretches for some length as far as Bishopsbourne. The overgrown cuttings and embankments support plants such as carline thistle, marjoram, hairy violet and cowslip. Warblers, such as the chiff-chaff, blackcap, willow warbler, lesser whitethroat and spotted flycatcher have all been recorded here, whilst glow-worms and bats made good use of this undisturbed habitat. The untouched borders of railways also enable plants such as the common buddleia and stinging nettle,

both attractive to butterflies, to thrive.

Beneath the huge arch it is worth pausing for a moment to consider the skill of the Victorian craftsmen. Look how the bricks are cleverly interlocked to produce a structure which has stood for well over a century.

Black Robin

At the main valley road is situated the Black Robin Inn (57). Here the old inn sign once bore the couplet:

'Rigden Dellman ales are sold Where once did live Black Robin bold'.

This referred to a notorious and particularly ruthless highwayman who terrorised private coaches making their way along the lonely Dover-Canterbury road in the early 18th century. From all accounts he would often mercilessly shoot the driver before demanding the occupants' valuables. He was eventually captured and hung on a roadside gibbet upon the bleak Barham Downs. A sad ending to this tale involves wicked Robin's horse who was

apparently so attached to his master, that it refused its fodder after the execution and starved itself to death.

Kingston

Between Kingston church (58) and the old railway bridge at Covet Lane, a footpath leads across a meadow. The Saxons first built the small parish church which is dedicated to St Giles. It was largely rebuilt in the 14th century and the tower is of the 15th century. There are some 14th-century wall

paintings, a 13th-century font and a Jacobean pulpit.

Once spelt Kingstone, it is considered that the name derives from the old Jutish kingdoms, but today it exists as little more than a quiet hamlet and never grew like other settlements along the valley. Some new housing has been added along The Street in recent decades, but the main features of interest are naturally associated with the church, its yew trees, old flint walls and homely cottages gathered around ❧

Barham church spire

chapter **six**
Country houses and parkland estates

Kingston - Bifrons Park

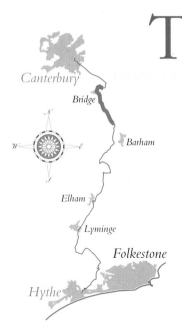

T he attractive open parklands of Charlton and Bourne with their grand mansions dominate this section. Their landscaped grounds show the ravages of the great storm of 1987, with fallen and wind-damaged trees, and newly planted trees to replace those lost. The tiny village of Bishopsbourne, perhaps the most unchanged in the valley, conjures up an image of old England with its village smithy, splendid church, public house, and cricket field. Meanwhile the larger and busier village of Bridge has a church, shops, and many fine pubs. The old railway trackbed lies hidden from view behind the majestic mansions in a cutting and a long tunnel

which both offer seclusion for an abundance of wildlife. The Nailbourne however is never very far away, even if you cannot see it!

Les beaux domaines de Charlton et de Bourne, avec leurs grandes demeures, dominent cette section. Leurs parcs paysagers témoignent des ravages de la grande tempête de 1987, par les arbres abattus ou abîmés par le vent, et les nouveaux arbres plantés en remplacement de ceux qui furent perdus. Le minuscule village de Bishopsbourne, sans doute le mieux conservé de la vallée, évoque l'Angleterre de jadis, avec sa forge, sa splendide église, son

pub et son terrain de cricket. Le village de Bridge, plus grand et plus animé, possède une église, des magasins et une quantité de jolis pubs. L'ancienne voie ferrée, derrière les majestueuses demeures, est dérobée à la vue par une tranchée et un long tunnel qui abritent une faune abondante. La Nailbourne, toutefois, n'est jamais bien loin, même si vous ne pouvez pas la voir!

Blacksmith, Bishopsbourne

Frozen lake at Bourne Park with tufted ducks

The countryside here is clearly different to the southern end of the valley. Fields for cultivation and grazing stretch out, whilst coniferous plantations spread to the west, but the dominant feature is parkland. The route of the old railway is mostly out of the valley because the railway contractors were obliged to dig deep into the gentle downs to pass behind the large estates at Charlton Park and Broome Park. The Nailbourne naturally takes the direct route between Bridge and Kingston, its water being used to feed ponds and lakes.

Charlton Park

Charlton Mansion (59) is seen through the trees to the south-west as this easily-walked section of the Elham Valley Way is followed. The building dates from the Tudor period, replacing an earlier house, but it was greatly extended in 1810 on the instructions of the Prince Regent (later George IV) in

Autumn colours

his dalliance with his mistress, Lady Elizabeth Conyngham of Bifrons, Patrixbourne. The interior is considered far more beautiful than the exterior with its fine panelling and decorations.

The parklands around Charlton (60), through which you walk, have likewise changed, especially during these past few years. New lime trees have replaced those brought down in the terrifying storm of 1987, although some older examples survive where sheep still graze on drooping

growth. Other trees have been pollarded and provide an excellent habitat for wildlife. Hole-nesting birds particularly are attracted to them and there are ample quantities of decaying woods for beetles, fungi and lichen, whilst pockets of dampness encourage ferns and other moisture-loving plants.

The Nailbourne's presence is also plainly evident, but nowadays it has much less impact on the area. Full use of the water was made in the original design of the park which featured ornamental lakes for swans, waterfalls and winding brooks, but today these are mostly dry; you will need to use your imagination in this instance! Since it is impossible to predict when the Nailbourne will flow, or how much water will run along its course and flood the fields, you never know whether you'll find a dried-up ditch or a surprisingly fast-running stream. If it is

the latter you may use a little bridge to keep your feet dry.

Bishopsbourne

Bishopsbourne lies in a quiet hollow and has remained a backwater ever since the road was diverted many years ago to meet up with the Dover Road high on Barham Downs. Former residents include the novelists Jocelyn Brook and Joseph Conrad. Conrad was a Pole, and originally a seafaring man until his love of rural Kent led him to forsake the oceans and seek the quiet reclusive life of a writer. He finally settled in 1919 at Oswalds (61), a delightful period house adjoining the church, where he spent his last five years. Between 1954 and 1970 Oswalds was the rectory.

Honeysuckle

Whereas most villages along the valley grew in population, Bishopsbourne declined and it is difficult to believe that in 1891 the local school once echoed to the sound of 45 pupils. Local trades once carried out here were of course associated with country life, and there were wheelwrights, carpenters, blacksmiths, bootmenders, farriers as well as a few small shops, a post office and a public house. The Mermaid Inn survives and a village blacksmith still carries on his trade through the demand for ornamental ironwork.

A short detour to the south-west will take you up the hill to where the old railway station is seen in a newly-cleared cutting. You may view the site from the iron bridge (but please respect privacy and resist trespassing onto the occupant's land). Here, the empty, trackless platforms curve northwards to Canterbury and it is difficult to imagine trains running through, let alone the days of the last war when a huge gun and its

complement of Royal Engineers were based here.

The deep, overgrown chalk cutting on the opposite side has thankfully been saved from planning applications for use as a rubbish tip. Today, its

House and lake, Bourne Park

dank and undisturbed interior has become an unofficial nature reserve, providing a useful refuge for wild plants, birds and animals. The disused tunnel at Bourne Park is also home to some of our native bats.

Bishopsbourne church (St Mary's) (62) dates back to the 13th century and has

been cared for by the owners of Bourne Park. A new tower was built in the late 15th century and has been cared for by the owners of Bourne Park. There are surviving medieval stalls,

floor tiles, stained glass and wall paintings. The west window is by Burne-Jones and William Morris. Outside, the graveyard contains many interesting headstones covered with ivy, whilst there is a peace and tranquillity about the place which is most attractive in this hectic age.

Bourne Park

The footpath between Bourne Park and Bishopsbourne meanders through pastures studded with clumps of trees and beech copses. In these high trees there are numerous rookeries, the noisy occupants of which wheel about the sky above you. Although the Elham Valley Way is enjoyable at all times of the year, there is something rather magical here in late autumn when these huge bare trees are magnificently silhouetted against a darkening sky.

The course of the Nailbourne is easily traced by the tell-tale line of damp-loving plants which grow along its length. Look out for, amongst others, watercress and fool's watercress, both edible but best avoided in case they carry the eggs of liverfluke, a parasitic flat worm which destroys the livers of sheep. The lake in front of Bourne House (63) supports water crowfoot (looks like a white buttercup) and amphibious bistort (whose name

Bishopsbourne station

accurately describes its contentedness for water or land).

Roman pottery and coins and also burials were unearthed during excavations for the lake in 1846, and more recently further research has indicated that this is probably the site of an important settlement.

Swallows and housemartins swoop for insects in summer, whilst the lapwing, with its wispy upright 'hairdo' and characteristic peooo-vit call, probes away on the wet short grassland.

Bourne Park (64) dates back to Domesday, but the house, known as Bourne Place until 1845, is of the Queen Anne

Period built in 1702, and considered to be the best specimen in Kent, with its superb front and rear elevations. Needless to say, the interior contains many impressive architectural features, including a Tudor fireplace from the original house which stood on the site. The Bell family, who lived here at the time of the railway's construction, objected to the prospect of seeing trains pass by from their rear windows. In order to appease, a 330-yard long tunnel (65) was provided where a normal cutting had been planned. A further concession involved provision of a station at Bishopsbourne where none had originally

been planned. Bourne Park also possessed one of the finest cricket pitches in the County and many memorable games are said to have been played here.

Evidence of far earlier inhabitation is scattered everywhere in this district. In the woods to the south there are numerous tumuli, which were all excavated during the last century. Roman remains were stumbled upon in the outskirts of Bridge where a burial ground was unearthed during excavations associated with improvements to Watling Street (66), the old Roman road between Canterbury and Dover.

Bridge Place (67) to the west of the Elham Valley Way is but a wing of a fine mansion built in the 17th century by a hapless Dover merchant, Sir Arnold Braems, who crippled himself financially with its construction. Today, the house is a country club. A little to the north, the Church of St Peter (68) sits among yews. This handsome

edifice contains a few Norman features although much of it was restored by Gilbert Scott in 1859-61.

Bridge

The village grew up around the crossing of the Nailbourne by the old Dover road, but you will be lucky to find any water flowing beneath the bridge which gives the place its name. For years, Bridge suffered the blight of heavy traffic, until the opening of the bypass gave the place back to the villagers who can now enjoy a more tranquil life.

Bridge contains some interesting old buildings, but most development has taken place in comparatively recent years, commencing to some extent with the arrival of the railway. However, the station on the old line was well over a mile away, tucked into the hillside to the west. A far older relic of times past once existed here, the village stocks, upon which the sobering motto was inscribed for foolish miscreants to contemplate:

View over Bishopsbourne

*'He who will not the law obey
Here in ye stocks must surely lay'.*

Once an important centre, Bridge headed a union of 25 surrounding parishes. There was also a workhouse here where the destitute and elderly might find work, shelter and medicine. Not surprisingly, its old inns once provided welcome overnight accommodation and refreshment for those who drove their carts and carriages on this centuries-old road between London and Dover.

Although the Elham valley line was prevented from serving the centre of the village, the usefulness of the railway was undeniable and from 1890 coal staithes were set up in the goods yard. This valuable commodity could henceforth be transported into the village far more easily when open fires and ranges were the sole means of heating. The railway was also beneficial to the local agricultural trade where the chief crops were wheat, barley, oats and hops.

The land around this area was more suited to hop gardens since the fragile bines could be sheltered from the winds which could ruin an entire harvest. Local people once would supplement their meagre incomes during the three-week hop-picking season, although this district never saw the vast numbers of Londoners who made the annual exodus into the Weald of Kent. Bridge also had a smock mill for grinding the local corn, but

the last remains of this were demolished in 1955.

Conyngham Lane connects the High Street with the Bifrons estate. During the last century, on the slopes of the downs to the east, a great many Saxon graves (69) were discovered when plantations on the Conyngham estate were laid out. Among them were the skeletons of men, most of whom were over six feet tall, and mothers who had died in childbirth, their pitiful little ones thoughtfully buried with them ❧

chapter seven
In the footsteps
of the pilgrims

Bifrons Park - Canterbury

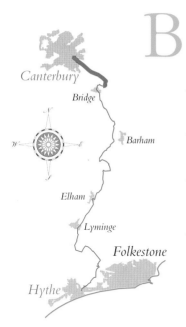

Canterbury

Bridge

N

W   E

S

Barham

Elham

Lyminge

Folkestone

Hythe

Bifrons Park with its mansion now in ruins has only avenues of limes and wellingtonias and ornate bridges to mark its previous position as one of the finer estates in the valley. However the neighbouring village of Patrixbourne provides one of the architectural gems of the valley, with timber-framed houses, many with carved corbels hovering discretely overhead, and a Norman church with beautiful stonework and intricate glass. A shaded, sunken byway connects the parkland landscape to the south with the more fertile agricultural belt which surrounds Canterbury. Old orchards have been grubbed up here and replaced with arable crops and modern smaller fruit trees, heavily laden with apples in late summer. Looking into the Stour valley, Canterbury, with its magnificent cathedral, dominates the view, as it has done for so many walkers in times past.

Bifrons Park, dont la demeure est aujourd'hui en ruine, n'a plus que ses allées de tilleuls et de wellingtonias et ses ponts très ornés comme témoins de l'époque où il comptait parmi les plus beaux domaines de la vallée. Le proche village de Patrixbourne est toutefois l'un des joyaux architecturaux de la vallée,

avec ses maisons à colombages, dont beaucoup ont en surplomb de discrets corbeaux sculptés, et son église de l'époque normande, à la belle maçonnerie en pierre et aux riches vitraux. Un chemin encaissé ombragé relie le paysage boisé, au sud, à la ceinture agricole plus fertile qui entoure Canterbury. Ici, les vieux vergers ont été déterrés et remplacés par des cultures arables et des petits arbres fruitiers modernes qui ploient sous les pommes à la fin de l'été. Face à la Stour Valley, Canterbury, avec sa magnifique cathédrale, domine la vue, comme elle l'a fait par le passé pour tant de randonneurs.

Ruins of St Augustine's Abbey, Canterbury

Bifrons Park

Bifrons Park (70) once possessed a magnificent mansion (72) which was originally constructed about 1600. It was remodelled in 1780 and again in the 19th century. In commendation of his wife, the owner placed a latin motto on the forefront which, translated, read:

'A good wife rebuilds that which has been destroyed, a bad wife destroys that which has been built up'.

The house had an identical double front, hence its latin name of Bifrons. It was bought in 1830 by the Marquess of Conyngham when he and the Marchioness were removed from the Royal Court following the death of King George IV. Evidently, the Marchioness was accused of having exercised unwelcome influence over the last King. Tragically, this handsome structure was lost in 1948 and if you are walking on the alternative route, you may gaze only upon a large hole in the ground to be greeted by the mournful, moss-covered ruins of its foundations. However, it takes little imagination, especially at dusk, to conjure up an image of the house in its heyday, full of light, laughter and music as numerous horse-drawn

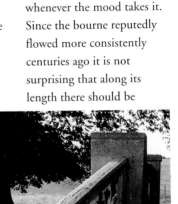
Ornamental bridge over the Nailbourne, Bifrons Park

carriages, bringing party guests, drew up on the gravelled drive. A gate lodge survives nearby and this displays 19th-century thatch and Tudoresque details which were based on Nash's Royal Lodge at Windsor for George IV. There is also an imposing avenue of graceful limes and wellingtonias.

The footpath running through the fields south of Patrixbourne will take you across the Nailbourne which flows through here seemingly whenever the mood takes it. Since the bourne reputedly flowed more consistently centuries ago it is not surprising that along its length there should be numerous sites of former habitation. Burial mounds and graves likewise once littered this district, providing evidence of early human habitation.

Patrixbourne

There used to be an old tale connected with Patrixbourne that on one night in the year, a procession of skeletons could be seen slowly walking round the church, sombrely led by a cowled monk.

Certainly, Kent seems to have more than its fair share of ghosts and spookish tales, but since this corner of England has been fought over, invaded, cultivated and lived in for thousands of years then it is, perhaps, not so surprising.

A rather quaint cottage may be seen bordering the Nailbourne near the church. It looks very typical of those depicted so cleverly in water colours by the Victorian artist Helen Allingham and probably fulfils most people's wistful longing for the ideal country hideaway. Nearby stands the Norman Church of St Mary's (71), built in flint and Caen stone and justly famous for its beautifully carved stonework and windows which can only be bettered in Kent by Barfrestone. The decoration on the elaborate south doorway is exceptionally fine. The rose or wheel window at the east end of the chancel is exquisite, whilst there are outstanding examples of medieval Flemish glass, as well as 18 panels of fine 16th

Wooded lane near Patrixbourne

and 17th-century Swiss glass donated by Lady Conyngham in 1837.

The vicarage bears the Conyngham crest and, if possible, time should be taken to explore this Kentish byway. Many of these striking houses possess ornate barge boards and sport carved wooden corbels which grimace at you from the eaves. Whilst the atmosphere is one of great antiquity, it comes as a surprise to learn that almost all of the Tudor designs were carved around the middle of the 19th century.

Patrixbourne also has two fords where the Nailbourne is thankfully left to flow across the road and there are numerous aspects and plentiful subjects to tempt artists and sketchers.

From here the Nailbourne heads north towards Bekesbourne, Littlebourne and Wickhambreaux, beyond which it finally flows into the Great Stour in the marshes near Sandwich. Running

Doorway, St Mary's Church, Patrixbourne

parallel is Station Road which leads to Bekesbourne station on the main Canterbury-Dover railway line, whilst a short distance further is Howletts Zoo Park, which is the home for a variety of exotic animals from many parts of the world.

The Elham Valley Way follows a leafy lane between the higher ground south-east of Canterbury and Patrixbourne, it also forms part of the North Downs Way. These ways are very typical of downland landscapes and create excellent linear habitats for a wide range of wildlife. Even though at this point you are

out of the designated Area of Outstanding Natural Beauty, the surrounding scenery has much to offer. Here, in springtime, wood anemones and celandines are dotted about on sunny banks and clumps of primroses similarly peep among the bursting greenery. You should also find the dainty wild violet, as well as a range of ferns, such as the hart's tongue which thrives on the damp, north-facing verges. In high summer a canopy of broad green leaves will shade you when the chance of a cool spot is welcome during such long, hot days.

Orchards

Between Hode Farm and Canterbury you will see orchards (73) on either side as the view extends over a wide area. Kent, famous for its fruit production, has soil and climate ideally suited for this purpose, its fertility once likened to the mythical Garden of Eden.

Gargoyle, cottage detail, Patrixbourne

Surprisingly, perhaps, the apple was not traditionally eaten by ordinary people since it was expensive and thus considered a luxury food. The original cultivars were introduced from Asia, whilst the Romans prized the fruit and reputedly served it on silver platters during their orgies! In the reign of Henry VIII, the first large-scale orchards were planted at Teynham, near Faversham, when the king's fruiter, Richard Harris, sought out the choicest varieties throughout the known world. Even in Queen Victoria's time the apple was still unaffordable and the common folk could only buy the windfalls and bruised, discarded leftovers. Famous Kent apples include the Beauty of Kent, Colonel Vaughan, Gascoyne's Scarlet, Kentish fillbasket, Sunset and Smart's Prince Arthur.

The traditional apple, pear, plum and cherry orchards, along with Kent cobnut platts, have disappeared due to incentives to grub, in order to produce more profitable orchards. The new and fewer intensively-managed modern dwarf rootstock orchards of apple and pear provide

Cottage detail, Patrixbourne

attractive spring blossom and autumn fruit, but they do not have the character, wildlife value, or ambience of the old orchards. The Countryside Commission, recognising old orchards have a value in the landscape and for wildlife, now offer payments to landowners to conserve them.

The lines of hybrid alders and poplars which protect the orchards from wind and frost are a distinctive feature in Kent and are more akin to landscapes of the near continent. Look out for the fruit-growers enemy, the brightly coloured bullfinch, which pecks away at springtide buds, as well as the tortoiseshell and red admiral butterflies which feed off nectar and rotten fruit.

If you are walking in the summer months you might be lucky enough to come across freshly-picked strawberries for sale.

The tradition of Londoners coming to Kent to pick fruit has all but ceased, but the old waymarked blossom trails, one of which crossed the Elham Valley Way between Littlebourne and Patrixbourne, are a sign that many colourful orchards in this area once buzzed with activity during the harvest.

East of Canterbury, the Elham Valley Way follows part of the old Pilgrims' Way (74) which runs from the east Kent coast at Ebbsfleet, near Ramsgate.

St Martin's Church

St Martin's Church (75) stands on the hill, quite close to the Elham Valley Way, on the eastern side of the city. This very early church is believed to be where St Augustine and his followers first worshipped on their

arrival in Canterbury in 597. The Venerable Bede, who wrote his History of the English Church and People in 730, believed that the original church was built during the period of Roman occupation. Some parts of the church are built entirely from Roman brick. This may be the church where Queen Bertha, the Christian wife of the pagan king Ethelbert worshipped before the arrival of the missionaries from Rome.

In the churchyard you will find many notable people buried, among them Thomas Sidney Cooper, 1803-1902, the famous Victorian painter.

He loved this place and painted innumerable pictures of cattle around the cathedral, the city and the Stour valley. Born in 1803 in Canterbury he studied under Eugene Verboeckhoven, the Belgian animal painter, and in 1833 he came into his own. He died in 1902 at 98 years of age.

Longport

On the opposite side of the road to St Martin's Church are the John and Ann Smith Almshouses (76). Mrs Ann Smith, when her husband died in 1656, gave a sum of money to found eight small cottages for four poor men and four poor women to live free of charge, *to page 74* ➡

Apple orchard

Canterbury

C anterbury is situated at the foot of the North Downs where the Great Stour flows west to east to the coast. Canterbury and the surrounding area has been occupied for more than 2,000 years. Archaeological excavations have shown that extensive Iron Age settlements existed on both sides of the Stour. Canterbury appears to have been the regional capital of the Cantiaci, and archaeological evidence suggests that trade routes were established along the downs to the coast and across the Channel.

Old Wife of Bath, Canterbury Tales

During the Roman period Canterbury was known as Durovernum Cantiacorum, and was the cantonal capital containing many fine public buildings including a forum and theatre, parts of both of which have been excavated. It was situated at an easy crossing point of the great Stour, and formed the hub of a network of Roman roads leading from the four ports of east Kent, at Reculver (Regulbium), Richborough (Rutupiae), Dover (Portus Dubris) and Lympne (Portus Lemanis). The Roman road from Richborough continued on through Canterbury to London (Londinium) and St Albans (Verulamium) and became known as Watling Street. This road pattern with Canterbury at its centre has basically remained the same to the present day, and was the major factor which made the city the nodal point of east Kent.

The Canterbury Cross is Anglo-Saxon and dated about AD 850. It was discovered in Canterbury during the last century and has since acquired widespread fame across the Anglican world as a symbol of the Church of Canterbury. It is made of bronze with applied silver panels and is on display in the Canterbury Heritage Museum.

In the early 5th century Roman military and civilian authority and administration collapsed. Settlement appears to have continued in parts of the city, with other areas becoming agricultural land. By the late 6th century, Canterbury was the capital of Ethelbert, the pagan king of Kent and regarded as the most important king as far north as Northumbria. His Christian wife, Bertha, continued to practice her own religion, probably in St Martin's Church. In 597 Augustine and 40 Christian missionaries arrived in Kent, and were given land outside the city walls where St Augustine's Abbey is now situated. Ethelbert was converted to Christianity and this was followed by a mass conversion of his subjects.

During the medieval period Canterbury developed as an important ecclesiastical centre, as well as a trading and commercial centre and, after the murder of Thomas à Becket in the cathedral in 1170, as a place of pilgrimage. In 1200 the city had an estimated population of 6,000. Many of the historic buildings seen in Canterbury today are of medieval date and construction and together comprise a third of all such buildings within Kent.

Canterbury Cathedral from the south-east

With the destruction of Becket's shrine and the dissolution of seven religious establishments in the city by Henry VIII between 1536-40, Canterbury lost its importance as a site of pilgrimage. There was a large influx of Walloon and Huguenot Protestant refugees from Europe in the 16th and 17th centuries. Many were weavers and the city gained a reputation for fine silk and later woollen cloth. In the late 18th century garrisons were established in the city, and soldiers accounted for about a third of the population.

By the 20th century Canterbury was a quiet market town. During the Second World War bombing raids destroyed much property, particularly in the area between Watling Street and Burgate on the south-east side of the city. More recently it has become a popular destination for tourists from the Continent ❧

and clergyman to provide a sermon for them every Sunday afternoon. This was all as a thanksgiving for the birth of a son after over twenty years of childless marriage. The gates of the almshouses show the date of 1657.

Near St Augustine's Abbey in Longport is Canterbury Prison (77) which was built in 1808 to the design by George Byfield. Mr William Prestley of Herne Bay, who was a brickmaker, helped to make the prison, and then later was put in there himself for smuggling. He died at the age of 101 years. The building was closed in 1920 and used for Foreign Office Archives. In 1921 it became a Naval Detention Barracks and then in 1946 used again as a prison.

Nearby is Barton Court (78), owned in the Middle Ages by the Abbot of St Augustine's. The present house was built in 1740 and is now a girls school. The last occupant of the house was Sir John Cecil

Russell, who came here in 1902. He had been in charge of the Mounted Infantry at

View of the West Gate from Westgate Gardens

Rorkes Drift in the Zulu War, and led his troops in the relief there in 1879.

The ruins of St Augustine's Abbey (79) are extensive remains of a medieval Benedictine abbey overlying ruins of earlier 7th and 11th century abbeys. Founded in 598 by St Augustine, the church was dedicated to Saints Peter and Paul in 613. The lower parts of the original church are constructed of Roman bricks and are still standing. Many other buildings were added to the complex in succeeding centuries. The abbey was dissolved in 1538 and many of the buildings were demolished although parts

remain in use today as a school. The great gateway of St Augustine's Abbey, or Fyndon Gate (81) at the eastern end of Lady Wootons Green, was built in 1300-9. The style of the period is Decorated with hints of Perpendicular. It was restored after bomb damage.

In Ivy Lane, which runs parallel with Longport, is a late 14th-century timber-framed house known as Old Hall (80). It is a typical Wealden-type hall house.

City walls

The remains of the great city walls (82) stand impressive. Begun long before the

Romans strengthened them, they were later rebuilt by the Normans who also set up 21 watch towers and six gates. Eight feet beneath you spread the Roman remains of ancient Canterbury and a portion of these are on exhibition. The walls were rebuilt in the 14th and 15th centuries in flint, and exactly follow the line of the Roman walls. The section alongside Broad Street is the most impressive length which survives. A partial arch of red Roman bricks among ragstone jambs can be seen to the left of the square bastion in the Queningate car park. It is the block-up remains of one of the Roman gateways (the Queningate).

River Stour and The Weavers, Canterbury

Burgate extends between the city walls and the magnificent Christ Church Gate. The Bur, Bar or Borough Gate (83), rebuilt of brick in 1475, stood at the entrance to Burgate. Most of the gateway was demolished in 1781, and the remaining tower in 1822. St George's Gate (84), the next one to the south-west, and which was rebuilt in 1470 (recent excavations revealed that it was similar in shape to West Gate), served as a defendable entry point to the city. The gateway was demolished in 1801.

Canterbury city centre

Following the bombing raids during the last war, the sole survivor in this area of the city is

the tower of St George's Church (85) where Marlowe, one of Canterbury's famous authors, was baptised in 1564. In Burgate is situated the isolated tower of St Mary Magdalene's Church (86) which was demolished in 1871. The tower was built in 1502 in the Perpendicular style of the period.

In Butchery Lane, underground, is preserved the remains of a Roman town house unearthed after the blitz of the Second World War with its hypocaust room

(heating system) and mosaic pavement. It forms the centre-piece of a new Roman Museum. Nearby in the High Street is the Cheques of Hope (88), an inn built by Prior Chillenden in the late 1390s to provide rest and refreshment for medieval pilgrims. The stone arches on the ground floor of the shop are all that remain of the hostelry which burnt down in 1860.

Christ Church Gateway (89) is an example of Perpendicular architecture built by Prior Goldstone between 1502 and 1519. The heraldry implies that it commemorates Prince Arthur, the elder brother of

Henry VIII, who died in 1502. The turrets having been removed in the 18th century were restored between 1937 and 1939. The gateway leads into the Cathedral precincts. The small square outside the gateway has been called Buttermarket for 200 years. Before then it was known as Bull Stake where bulls were baited by dogs before slaughter in the belief that the beef would then have a better flavour.

Canterbury Cathedral

The breath-taking beauty of Christ Church Cathedral, Canterbury (90) may be equally appreciated at close quarters or from the hills that surround the city. It is the seat of the Archbishop of Canterbury, Primate of All England. It occupies the site of a

Stained glass window, Canterbury Cathedral

humble church established by St Augustine, the first Archbishop of Canterbury. Ransacked and fired by the Danes in 1011, the original building lay in ruins until repaired by King Canute, but yet again, in 1067, it was burned to the ground. In 1070 Archbishop Lanfranc set to work upon a stone structure, but it took almost 400 years of alterations and rebuilding to achieve what you see today. The great central or Bell Harry, tower was constructed in 1495 and rises 234 feet in height, whilst the twin western towers are equally impressive. As you look at the western elevation the tower on the right pre-dated Bell Harry by 50 years, whilst the left hand tower is relatively new, replacing the Arundel steeple in 1840. The principal features are the Norman crypt, the site of Thomas à Becket's shrine, the tombs of Henry IV (died 1413) and Edward the Black Prince (died 1376), the 12th-century choir and 14th-century screen. Recent archaeological excavations, carried out in 1993 in the nave, have revealed the remains of what may be part of the original church of St Augustine with foundations of re-used Roman stone, with mortared stone and Roman bricks above. In addition a substantial part of the later Anglo-Saxon cathedral, including part of a hexagonal tower, of the 9th and 10th centuries has been discovered.

The King's School now occupying the ancient building of the Christ Church monastery and one of the oldest scholastic foundations in England, is noted for its fine exterior Norman staircase (91).

Palace Street

St Alphege Church (92) was built soon after Archbishop Lanfranc realigned Palace Street to make way for his new palace opposite. It is used today as the Canterbury Urban Studies Centre. Conquest House (93) has a 17th-century half-timbered front with a 12th-century crypt where, traditionally, the four knights plotted to murder Thomas à Becket. The front room, now a shop, has a coat of arms of Charles I above the fireplace.

It is, perhaps, entirely appropriate that the journey on foot along the Elham Valley Way should either begin or finish at Canterbury Cathedral. The ancient city is a centre of pilgrimage for visitors, tourists and sightseers. No other place in Kent can rival what it has to offer, and there exists within its glorious vaulted expanse an enduring sense of timelessness. It is one of the finest monuments in the Christian world, but you may equally find this sense of peace and time stood still in many places along the Elham Valley Way. The intimate, quiet fields and meadows along the rural byways or the wide, open, breezy heights of the downs all possess their own special atmosphere. Relish this walk and the scenery along the way, surely some of Kent's finest ❧

St Augustine of Canterbury

'Non Angli sed angeli' (not English but angels) the future Pope Gregory VI said on seeing his first English in a Constantinople slave market. And so it came to pass that when he became Pope of all Christendom, he made it his business to send his companion of that day, one Augustine, to bring salvation to pagan England.

Christianity had gained a foothold in Britain during the Roman occupation some centuries earlier but most of its supporters had been driven to the far corners of the country by the heathen Anglo-Saxon invaders. Augustine began his mission in Kent not only because of its ease of access from continental Europe; Bertha, Frankish wife of Ethelbert, king of Kent,

was already a Christian and her chaplain Bishop Liudhard had requested help from Gregory in spreading the Word.

Augustine and his 40 companions landed near the Isle of Thanet early in 597 and proceeded to Canterbury, carrying a silver cross and praying aloud to their God. Ethelbert greeted him with some reserve, but afforded the missionaries good lodgings, near the existing Christian

church of St Martin. Within the year, the king was so impressed by their teachings that he was baptised and became a Christian.

Following their king's example, some 10,000 of his subjects were baptised on Christmas Day, 597.

Augustine died in 604 and was buried in the abbey he had set up outside the city walls. In his brief seven years as Archbishop of Canterbury, he established Christianity as

the official religion, developed an efficient church administration, built a priory where the present cathedral stands. Within a few generations, much of England had been converted to Christianity.

St Augustine: Mission of Faith Stamps

Two Royal Mail postage stamps commemorating this noted Christian saint were issued on 11 March 1997.

The design of the 43p value stamp features St Augustine blessing the king of Kent; on the 63p denomination he is shown as the founder of Canterbury Cathedral.

The stamps mark the 1400th anniversary of the arrival of St Augustine in Britain &

Reproduced by permission of the Post Office

Elham Valley
Exploring the area

Interesting places to visit

On or near the Elham Valley Way

St Leonards Church crypt
Church Road, Hythe

Hythe Local History Room
Stade Street, Hythe
Tel: Hythe (01303) 266152

Romney, Hythe and Dymchurch Railway
Hythe
Tel: New Romney (01679) 62553

Port Lympne Wild Animal Park, Mansion and Garden
Lympne
Tel: Hythe (01303) 264647

Sandgate Castle
Sandgate, Folkestone
Tel: Folkestone (01303) 221881

Metropole Arts Centre
The Leas, Folkestone,
Tel: Folkestone (01303) 244706

Folkestone Museum and Art Gallery
Grace Hill, Folkestone
Tel: Folkestone (01303) 850123

Martello Tower No. 3 Visitor Centre
East Cliff, Folkestone
Tel: Folkestone (01303) 242113

Elham Valley Railway Exhibition
Peene, Folkestone
Tel: Folkestone (01303) 252335

Hornbeam in Covert Wood at springtime

Parsonage Farm Rural
Heritage Centre
North Elham, Canterbury
Tel: Elham (01303)
840766

Elham Valley Vineyards
Breach, Barham, Nr
Canterbury
Tel: Canterbury (01227)
831266

Howletts Zoo Park
Bekesbourne, Canterbury
Tel: Canterbury (01227)
721410

St Augustine's Abbey
Longport, Canterbury
Tel: Canterbury (01227)
767345

Christ Church Cathedral
Canterbury
Tel: Canterbury (01227)
762862

Roman Museum
Butchery Lane, Canterbury
Tel: Canterbury (01227)
452747

Canterbury Tales
St Margaret's Street,
Canterbury
Tel: Canterbury (01227)
454888

Canterbury Centre
St Alphege Lane,
Canterbury
Tel: Canterbury (01227)
457009

Royal Museum and Art
Gallery
High Street, Canterbury
Tel: Canterbury (01227)
452747

Canterbury Heritage
Museum
Stour Street, Canterbury
Tel: Canterbury (01227)
452747

West Gate Museum
St Peter's Street, Canterbury
Tel: Canterbury (01227)
452747

Parish churches
*(keys usually obtained locally
if not open)*

**Countryside open
spaces**
*on or near the Elham Valley
Way*

Royal Military Canal
Hythe

Folkestone Downs
Folkestone
Tel: Folkestone (01303)
274806

Brockhill Country Park
Saltwood, Hythe
Tel: Hythe (01303)
258594

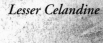

Lesser Celandine

Other walking opportunities

If you have enjoyed this walk and would like to explore other waymarked walking routes in Kent, write to the Access and Recreation Officer (listed elsewhere) for a publications catalogue.

It is possible for you to devise your own shorter linear and circular walks using the extensive rights of way network throughout the county. Information about these can be obtained by studying either the Ordnance Survey Explorer maps or the Kent County Council Definitive Maps of Public Rights of Way. Copies of the latter can be inspected at public libraries or district council offices. In the event of difficulty please contact the Public Rights of Way Manager (listed elsewhere).

Linked, or running close, to the Elham Valley in Kent are a number of other walks, as follows:

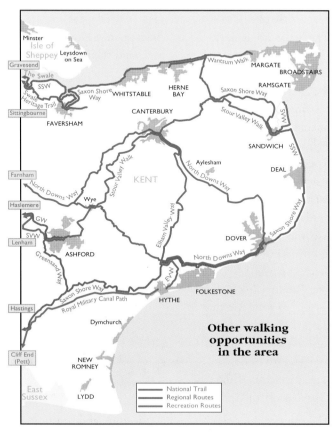

Other walking opportunities in the area

North Downs Way

Valued for its dramatic south-facing escarpment, secluded dry valleys, network of tiny lanes, isolated farms and churches, the North Downs are the backbone of the Kent and Surrey landscape rising between the capital and coast, seen by millions using the railways and motorways which skirt the boundaries.

Ancient woods, unimproved grasslands, scattered oast houses and small orchards provide a rich tapestry of wildlife habitats of international nature conservation importance and a legacy of sites of historic interest.

The North Downs Way National Trail explores this special landscape along 153 miles of waymarked paths linking the White Cliffs of Dover to Farnham in Surrey.

Publications:
North Downs Way National Trail Guide - Neil Curtis, Aurum Press, 25 Bedford Avenue, London WC1B 3AT and Orndance Survey, Romsey Road, Southhampton, Hampshire SO9 4DH

North Downs Way, - A Users' Handbook - Kent County Council, Planning Department, Springfield, Maidstone, Kent ME14 2LX.

Saxon Shore Way

The Saxon Shore Way, running for 163 miles from Gravesend in Kent round the ancient coastline to Hastings in east Sussex, offers the long-distance walker an unrivalled diversity of scenery. The Way follows the wide expanses of marshland bordering the Thames and Medway estuaries and the White Cliffs of Dover. There are panoramic views over Romney Marsh from the escarpment that marks the ancient coastline between Folkestone and Rye, and from the sandstone cliffs of the High Weald at Hastings.

The route is also rich in historical sites and literary associations. Here the Romans invaded Britain and, later, built the Saxon Shore forts to defend the island against a new wave of invaders. Here St Augustine landed to bring the Gospel to the Anglo-Saxon Kingdom which would later fall to the Normans who, in their turn, erected great fortresses like Dover Castle to defend their conquests.

The shore line is of interest to the naturalist because of its importance

Looking through Yalding Bridge - Greensand Way (County Visuals)

as a feeding and roosting place for wintering and migratory birds.

Publication:
Saxon Shore Way Recreational Path Guide - Bea Cowan, Aurum Press/ Ordnance Survey/ Kent County Council - Kent County Council, Planning Department, Springfield, Maidstone, Kent ME14 2LX.

Greensand Way

The Greensand Way, as its name implies, follows the Greensand ridge across Surrey and Kent, between Haslemere and Hamstreet, and provides a long-distance walking route of about 108 miles across some of the most attractive country in south-east England.

From Haslemere the Way passes the Devils Punchbowl and crosses Hascombe Hill and Winterfold Heath to Pitch, Holmbury and Leith Hills. From here it descends to Dorking and continues eastwards via Reigate Heath, Bletchingly, Tandridge and Limpsfield Chart.

In Kent it crosses Toys' and Ide Hills before descending through pastures to Sevenoaks Weald, continues through Knole Park to Ightham Mote, and crosses the Medway valley to Yalding.

The route quickly ascends the ridge and passes through the villages of Linton, Sutton Valence, Ulcombe and Egerton through orchards and hop gardens with many panoramic views over the Weald to the south.

The ridge becomes indistinct beyond Great Chart but the route crosses a rolling landscape of farmland and woodland. The Greensand Way eventually joins the Saxon Shore Way at Hamstreet.

Publication:
Along and around the Greensand Way - Bea Cowan, Kent and Surrey County Councils in association with

Chilham Mill - Stour Valley Walk (County Visuals)

Ordnance Survey - Kent County Council, Planning Department, Springfield, Maidstone, Kent ME14 2LX.

Stour Valley Walk

Walk across east Kent along the valley of the River Stour from the source of the river at Lenham to the sea at Pegwell Bay. Passing through a varied but consistently attractive landscape, this 51½-mile route takes in downland, woodland, orchards, hop gardens, lakes, dykes and marshland, unspoilt villages and historic towns.

Between Lenham and Ashford the route passes through fertile farmland, Hothfield Common and Victoria Park. North of Ashford, the walker has an inviting prospect of the North Downs to the north. The route continues through a gap in the downs.

Further on, the City of Canterbury is a worthwhile stop for its places of historic and archaeological interest. East of Canterbury is Fordwich, the limit, in medieval times, of the navigable section of the river.

The remainder of the route traces the old Saxon shoreline of the Wantsum Channel to the important Roman site at Richborough, thence to the ancient Cinque Port of Sandwich, and the sea at Pegwell Bay.

Publication:
Stour Valley Walk - Veronica Litten, Kent County Council, Planning Department, Springfield, Maidstone, Kent ME14 2LX.

Wantsum Walk

This linear coastal walk running for eight miles between Herne Bay and Birchington is historically one of the most interesting in the whole area. Comprising a cliff-top path and sea wall, it passes through the ancient site of Reculver and crosses the northern end of the former Wantsum Channel which separated the Isle of Thanet from the mainland up to medieval times. The coastline is also of outstanding interest for its geological and natural history value, as seen in the cliffs and seashore, and in the marshes and dykes behind the sea wall.

Linking with this linear walk are two circular walk networks which have been developed between the coast and Upstreet and Sarre respectively.

Publication:
Coastal Walks in Kent - Wantsum Walks - Kent County Council, Planning Department, Springfield, Maidstone, Kent ME14 2LX.

Circular Walks on the Saxon Shore Way - Brockhill Country Park

Linked to the Saxon Shore Way and centred on Brockhill Country Park is a network of three circular walks ranging between three and six miles in length.

The Brockhill walks visit the North Downs, a section of the Royal Military Canal and Saltwood village. There are fine views overlooking Romney Marsh to the sea beyond.

Publication:
Brockhill Country Park -
Circular Walks on the
Saxon Shore Way -
Kent County Council,
Planning Department,
Springfield, Maidstone,
Kent ME14 2LX.

Folkestone, Hythe and Elham Valley Walks

Discover the lovely
countryside of the Elham
valley with the Folkestone,
Hythe and Elham Valley
Walks Pack, which contains
all the details you need for
12 individual walks, all
accessible by public
transport, ranging in length
from one to seven miles.
In addition the pack
includes three landscape
detective cards to explain
about the history and
wildlife of the countryside.

Publication:
Folkestone, Hythe and
Elham Valley Walks -
White Cliffs Countryside
Project, Countryside
Management Centre,
Castle Hill, Folkestone,
Kent CT19 4AJ.

Circular Walks around Elham

If you choose to spend a
little time in the village of
Elham there is plenty of
opportunity to walk on the
local footpaths around the
village. Before you step
out, pop into one of the
village shops to pick up
one of the two Elham
Walks packs. Each pack
contains four walks based
around the village with full
route directions and points
of interest along the way.
All profits from the Elham
walks go to the New
Village Hall fund.

Publication:
Elham Walks - Elham
Village Hall Association

c/o Mr & Mrs J Neumark,
Cycleways, New Road,
Elham, Canterbury, Kent.

The Magic of Romney Marsh

The Romney Marsh
Countryside Project
(RMCP) has produced a
walks pack entitled The
Magic of Romney Marsh
with funding from Shepway
District Council and the
Rural Development
Commission.

The pack contains a
beautiful colour folder
enclosing nine self-guided
laminated walk cards. Each
of the walks are themed
with a sketch map
surrounded with delightful
artwork, along with
detailed route directions
and plenty of fascinating
information for the walker
to discover.

Fifty-one miles of fun on
the Romney Marsh. Follow
the paths of the Railway
Children in the landscape
of Edith Nesbit. Brave the
Countryside of Dr Syn and
find out who are the Saints
and Sinners on the Marsh.
Discover The Ingoldsby
Legends or have an Apple
Danish on your travels.

Publication:
The Magic of Romney
Marsh - Romney Marsh
Countryside Project,
Romney Resource Centre,
Mountfield Road, New
Romney, Kent TN28 8LH.

Royal Military Canal (County Visuals)

Further information and references

Bibliography

Britain's Natural Heritage
P Coleburn & R Gibbons

Buildings of England (The)
North East and East Kent
J Newman
Penguin

St Augustine's Abbey, Canterbury

Canterbury Cathedral
*Pages 1-4 in Canterbury's
Archaeology 1992-93*
K Blockley & P Bennett
Canterbury Archaeological
Trust

Discovering Canterbury:
A geographical and
historical guide to the city
H Mountford
Christ Church College,
Canterbury

Downland Wildlife
J Burton & J Davis

Elham Valley Line (The)
Brian Hart
Wild Swan Publications

Elham Valley Reflections
Brian Hart
Millgate Publishing

History of the Countryside
(The)
O Rackham
Weidenfeld and Nicolson Ltd

Hythe Haven -
The story of the town
and Cinque Port of Hythe
D Forbes
Shearwater Press, Hythe

Royal Military Canal (The)
P A L Vine
David and Charles

Local information and free
leaflets, plus a series of self-
guided walks around the
Folkestone, Hythe and
Elham Valley area are
available from the White
Cliffs Countryside Project.

Countryside Access Charter

Your rights of way are:

- Public footpaths - on foot only.

- Bridleways - on foot, horseback and pedal cycle.

- Byways - (usually old roads), most roads used as public paths and, of course public roads - all traffic.

Use maps, signs and waymarks. Ordnance Survey Pathfinder and Landranger maps show most public rights of way.

Signpost, North Downs Way

On rights of way you can:

- Take a pram, pushchair or wheelchair if practicable.

- Take a dog (on a lead or under close control).

- Take a short route round an illegal obstruction or remove it sufficiently to get past.

You have a right to go for recreation to:

- Public parks and open spaces - on foot.

- Most commons near older towns and cities - on foot and sometimes on horseback.

- Private land where the owner has a formal agreement with the local authority.

In addition you can use the following by local or established custom or consent - ask for advice if you are unsure:

- Many areas of open country like moorland, fell and coastal areas, especially those of the National Trust, and most commons.

- Some woods and forests, especially those owned by the Forestry Commission.

- Country parks and picnic sites.

- Most beaches.

- Towpaths on canals and rivers.

- Some land that is being rested from agriculture, where notices allowing access are displayed.

- Some private paths and tracks.

Consent sometimes extends to riding horses and pedal cycles.

For your information

- County and metropolitan district councils and London boroughs have a duty to protect, maintain and record rights of way, and hold registers of commons and village greens - report problems you find to them.

- Obstructions, dangerous animals, harassment and misleading signs on rights of way are illegal.

- If a public path runs along the edge of a field, it must not be ploughed or disturbed.

- A public path across a field can be ploughed or

disturbed to cultivate a crop, but the surface must be quickly restored and the line of the path made apparent on the ground.

- Crops (other than grass) must not be allowed to inconvenience the use of a rights of way, or prevent the line from being apparent on the ground.

- Landowners can require you to leave land to which you have no right of access.

- Motor vehicles are normally permitted only on roads, byways and some roads used as public paths.

- Follow any local bylaws.

And, wherever you go, follow the Country Code:

This Charter is for practical guidance in England and Wales only. Fuller advice is given in a free booklet 'Out in the Country' available from Countryside Commission Postal Sales, PO Box 124, Walgrave, Northampton NN6 9TL, telephone (01604) 781848. Published with kind permission of the Countryside Commission ↝

Country Code

Enjoy the countryside and respect its life and work

❧

Guard against all risk of fire

❧

Fasten all gates

❧

Keep your dogs under close control

❧

Keep to public paths across farmland

❧

Use gates and stiles to negotiate fences, hedges and walls

❧

Leave livestock, crops and machinery alone

❧

Take your litter home Help to keep all water clean

❧

Protect wildlife, plants and trees

❧

Take special care on country roads

❧

Make no unnecessary noise

Table of historical periods

Mesolithic	10000	-	3500BC
Neolithic	3500	-	2000BC
Bronze Age	2000	-	800BC
Iron Age	800BC	-	AD43

Prehistoric

Roman	43	-	410
Anglo Saxon	410	-	1066
Norman	1066	-	1154

Plantagenet	1154	-	1399
Lancastrian	1399	-	1461
Yorkist	1461	-	1485

Medieval

Tudor	1485	-	1603
Elizabethan	1558	-	1603

Renaissance

Stuart	1603	-	1714
Jacobean	1603	-	1649
Commonwealth	1649	-	1660
Restoration	1660	-	1702
Queen Anne	1702	-	1714

Hanoverian	1714	-	1901
Georgian	1714	-	1837
Regency	1810	-	1820
Victorian	1837	-	1901

Edwardian	1901	-	1910
Windsor	1910	-	Present day

Table of architectural periods

Romanesque	1066	-	1190

Early English	1190	-	1280
Decorated	1280	-	1380
Perpendicular	1380	-	1550

Gothic

Classical	1550	-	1810
Gothic & Classical Revivals	1810	-	1914
Modern	1914	-	Present day

Index

Key

Guidebook
Red = text
Blue = illustrations
Route guide
Green = text
Black = illustrations

Biographies

John Cann

John Cann has lived and worked by the sea at Whitstable for many years. He feels strongly about the Kent landscape and coastal scene and is fascinated by the way that the historical events have shaped the County and its people.

His paintings have very much evolved from a relationship with this environment. He has undertaken numerous private and public commissions and exhibited his watercolours and oil paintings in England, Germany and France.

John Cann has been involved in producing and illustrating many books using his drawings to interpret the past and to create an understanding and appreciate of the present.

Tim Fagan

Tim Fagan was born in London and moved to east Kent as a child at the beginning of the 1960s when it was still very rural. He fell in love with the place and has been exploring it ever since.

After an art-based education, he began to photograph aspects of the landscape that culminated in three exhibitions for Kent Arts and Libraries: Hidden Kent - 1985, Change and Decay - 1987 and Writers' Kent - 1989.

Married to a painter, he now lives near Canterbury and works as a technical assistant at Canterbury College of Art.

Brian Hart

Brian Hart was born in 1949 at Cheriton and spent much of his childhood exploring the locality covered by the Elham Valley Way.

His prime interest is the development of Kent's railways and the impact they had on local communities. He is wellknown for having written a number of authoritative railway histories including books on the Elham Valley Line, the Hythe and Sandgate Branch and the Canterbury and Whitstable Railway.

Although he now lives in the Weald of Sussex, 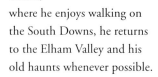 where he enjoys walking on the South Downs, he returns to the Elham Valley and his old haunts whenever possible.

Philip Rutt

Philip Rutt was born in Folkestone in 1956 and has lived and worked in the area since that time. The landscape and wildlife of Kent has formed the basis for much of his artwork.

He trained as a designer rather than a fine artist and his technical abilities and attention to detail has made his work very popular with specialists.

Philip has established a successful business producing environmental interpretation material for various organisations both in England and overseas.

On the rare occasions when not working, Philip enjoys country walks with his family.